MILITARY UNITS AND FORMATIONS OF THE ROYAL NAVY IN WORLD WAR II

Books LLC®, Wiki Series, Memphis, USA, 2011. ISBN: 9781156680476. www.booksllc.net
Copyright: http://creativecommons.org/licenses/by-sa/3.0/deed.en

Table of Contents

14th/17th Minesweeper Flotilla 1
1st Aircraft Carrier Squadron (Royal Navy) 2
2nd Battle Squadron (United Kingdom) 2
2nd Escort Group (Royal Navy) 2
36th Escort Group (Royal Navy) 4
3rd Battle Squadron (United Kingdom) 5
5th Escort Group (Royal Navy) 5
700 Naval Air Squadron 6
750 Naval Air Squadron 7
792 Naval Air Squadron 8
835 Naval Air Squadron 8
Allied Technical Air Intelligence Unit 10
B-2 Escort Group (Royal Navy) 11
B-6 Escort Group (Royal Navy) 12
B-7 Escort Group (Royal Navy) 13
Battlecruiser Squadron (United Kingdom) 14
British Pacific Fleet 15
Eastern Fleet 18
Escort Group (naval) 22
Force H 22
Force K 24
Force Z 25
Home Fleet 25
List of Eastern Fleet ships 27
Mediterranean Fleet 27

Introduction

Purchase of this book entitles you to a free trial membership in the publisher's book club at www.booksllc.net. (Time limited offer.) Simply enter the barcode number from the back cover onto the membership form. The book club entitles you to select from hundreds of thousands of books at no additional charge. You can also download a digital copy of this and related books to read on the go. Simply enter the title or subject onto the search form to find them.

Each chapter in this book ends with a URL to a hyperlinked online version. Type the URL exactly as it appears. If you change the URL's capitalization it won't work. Use the online version to access related pages, websites, footnotes, tables, color photos, updates. Click the version history tab to see the chapter's contributors. Click the edit link to suggest changes.

A large and diverse editor base collaboratively wrote the book, not a single author. After a long process of discussion and debate, the chapters gradually took on a neutral point of view reached through consensus. Additional editors expanded and contributed to chapters striving to achieve balance and comprehensive coverage. This reduced the regional or cultural bias found in many other books and provided access and breadth on subject matter otherwise little documented.

14th/17th Minesweeper Flotilla

The **14th/17th Minesweeper Flotilla** was a Royal Navy minesweeper flotilla based in Malta during the Second World War.

History
The flotilla comprised four fleet minesweepers from the Devonport based 14th M/S Flotilla – two *Halcyon* class (HMS *Speedy* and HMS *Hebe*) and two *Bangor* class (HMS *Rye* and HMS *Hythe*).

The four vessels were detached from 14th M/S Flotilla in 1942 and designated 17th M/S Flotilla on arrival in Gibraltar. The flotilla commander was Cdr Doran RN in HMS *Speedy*.

The flotilla proceeded to Malta in June 1942 as part of the Malta Convoy Operation *Harpoon*. The four sweepers cleared the approaches to Grand Harbour and led the *Harpoon* convoy into Malta. During its service in Malta the flotilla was known as 14th/17th Minesweeper Flotilla. The flotilla participated in the famous Malta Convoy Operation *Pedestal* during August 1942, which included the rescue of the oil tanker SS *Ohio*, for which Lt J. A. Pearson of HMS *Rye* was awarded the DSC.

14th/17th Minesweeper Flotilla, Malta, August 1942
- HMS *Speedy* - Lt Cdr J. C. Brooks RN
- HMS *Hebe* (J 24) - Lt Cdr G. Mowatt RN
- HMS *Rye* (J 76) - A/Lt Cdr J. A. Pearson RNR
- HMS *Hythe* (J 194) - Lt Cdr L. B. Miller RN
- Commander Minesweepers Malta, Cdr J. J. Jerome RN, also in HMS *Speedy*

Source (edited): "http://en.wikipedia.org/wiki/14th/17th_Minesweeper_Flotilla"

1st Aircraft Carrier Squadron (Royal Navy)

The **1st Aircraft Carrier Squadron** was a group of Royal Navy aircraft carriers assigned to the British Pacific Fleet in November 1944. They were HMS *Formidable*, *Indomitable*, *Victorious*, *Illustrious* and *Indefatigable*.

While serving in the Pacific, within the U.S. Fifth Fleet, the squadron was designated "Task Group 57.2".

During operations off Okinawa, the squadron received heavy Kamikaze attacks. Their armoured flight decks were adequate protection for the hangar decks, but the stress caused deformation of the ships' structures.

Source (edited): "http://en.wikipedia.org/wiki/1st_Aircraft_Carrier_Squadron_(Royal_Navy)"

2nd Battle Squadron (United Kingdom)

The British Royal Navy **2nd Battle Squadron** was a naval squadron consisting of battleships. The 2nd Battle Squadron was initially part of the Royal Navy's Grand Fleet. After World War I the Grand Fleet was reverted back to its original name, the Atlantic Fleet. The squadron changed composition often as ships were damaged, retired or transferred.

August 1914

On 5 August 1914, the squadron was constituted as follows:
- - HMS *King George V*
- HMS *Ajax*
- HMS *Audacious*
- HMS *Centurion*
- HMS *Conqueror*
- HMS *Monarch*
- HMS *Orion*
- HMS *Thunderer*

Battle of Jutland, June 1916

As an element in the Grand Fleet, the Squadron participated in the Battle of Jutland. During the Battle of Jutland, the composition of the 2nd Battle Squadron was as follows:
- **First Division**
- HMS *King George V* Flagship of Vice Admiral Sir Martyn Jerram; Captain F. L. Field;
- HMS *Ajax* Captain G. H. Baird;
- HMS *Centurion* Captain M. Culme-Seymour;
- HMS *Erin* Captain the Honourable V. A. Stanley;
- **Second Division**
- HMS *Orion* Flagship of Rear Admiral A. C. Leveson; Captain O. Backhouse;
- HMS *Monarch* Captain G. H. Borrett;
- HMS *Conqueror* Captain H. H. D. Tothill;
- HMS *Thunderer* Captain J. A. Fergusson.

January 1918

By 1918, HMS *Agincourt* had been transferred from the 1st Battle Squadron.

September 1939

By this time the squadron was in the Home Fleet and consisted of:
- - HMS *Royal Oak* Flagship of Rear Admiral H. E. C. Blagroven; Captain W.G. Benn;
- HMS *Royal Sovereign* Captain L. V. Morgan;
- HMS *Ramilies* Captain H. T. Baillie-Grohman;
- HMS *Nelson* Captain G. J. A. Miles;
- HMS *Rodney* Captain E. N. Syfret.

Source (edited): "http://en.wikipedia.org/wiki/2nd_Battle_Squadron_(United_Kingdom)"

2nd Escort Group (Royal Navy)

The **2nd Escort Group** (2 EG) was a British anti-submarine formation of the Royal Navy which saw action during the Second World War, principally in the Battle of the Atlantic.

2 EG was formed in April 1943, one of five such support groups formed at the crisis point of the campaign. It was to act as reinforcement to convoys under attack, with the capacity to actively hunt and destroy U-boats, rather than be restricted to escort duties. Comprising six sloops of the *Black Swan*-class, the group was led by Captain F.J. "Johnnie" Walker, Britain's most successful anti-submarine warfare commander, in *Starling*. The combination of an active hunting group and a charismatic, determined and innovative anti-submarine specialist such as Walker proved to be a potent force; 2 SG was the most successful anti-submarine unit of the war, being credited with the destruction of 23 U-boats during two years of active service.

Formation

Officially called 2nd Escort Group, (more commonly referred as the 2 SG) was formed in April 1943, one of five such groups. Its purpose was to provide reinforcement to convoys at sea, being equipped to spend extended periods at sea moving from one convoy to another as needed. Its function primarily was to assist a convoys escort in its defence, though it also had the facility to spend time, which escorts did not have, to continue attacks on U-boats to successful conclusion rather than having to break off to maintain the guard on the convoy. Walker however was determined that the group would be active in destroying U-boats and impressed this aim on his commanders from the outset.

The group comprised six sloops of

the Black Swan class, making it a highly uniform group, and the sloop design was well suited to the task, with good endurance, adequate speed and specialized anti-submarine armament. In addition Walker had developed a range of A/S tactics, which 2 SG became adept at, such as the "creeping attack" and the "barrage attack".

The group originally comprised:
- *Starling* (Capt. F.J. Walker),
- *Wren* (Cdr. R.M. Aubrey),
- *Woodpecker* (Lt.Cdr. R.E.S. Hugonin),
- *Cygnet* (Lt.Cdr. F.B. Proudfoot),
- *Wild Goose* (Lt.Cdr. D.E.G. Wemyss),
- *Kite* (Lt.Cdr. W.F. Segrave)

During April the group was engaged in working up and training; *Starling*, *Wild Goose* and *Kite* were new ships, and none had worked together before. Under Walkers training (previously the Experimental Commander at HMS *Osprey*, the RN Anti-submarine training school) the group became a highly effective and successful unit.

History

First patrols

The group's first patrol in May 1943 was uneventful. There were several major convoy battles during the month, but none involving 2 SG. The group operated in support of HX 235 and ONS 8, sailing ahead in an attempt to encounter and breach any U-boat patrol lines drawn across the convoy routes.

The group's first success came in June. Its first U-boat was detected on 1 June 1943: fortuitously on a fine day, and identified by a Lt. Earl Howe Pitt, the event was dubbed another "Glorious First of June" by Walker. Over a 15-hour period the group found, tracked and destroyed *U-202*, in the longest hunt of the Atlantic campaign up to that point, and a vindication of the support group ethos, leaving ships free of escort responsibilities to destroy U-boats.

Bay offensive

After a refit at Liverpool, after which *Cygnet* departed to another group, 2SG was assigned to "Operation Musketry", an attempt in concert with Coastal Command to interdict the U-boat transit routes across the Bay of Biscay. On 24 June 1943 the group was successful in destroying *U-119* and *U-449*, though *Starling* was damaged in the process of ramming *U-119* and was forced to retire. Walker elected to stay with the group, exchanging commands with *Wild Goose*, and, after the group returned to port, with *Kite*. 2 SG was joined at this point by *Woodcock* (Lt.Cdr C. Gwinner), as replacement for the damaged *Starling*.

On 30 July 1943 Walker's group saw further success when they encountered a group of three U-boats on the surface (two were vital submarine type XIV replenishment boats known as "Milk Cows") while in the Bay of Biscay. He signalled the "general chase" to his group and fired at them, causing damage that prevented them from diving. Two of the submarines, *U-462*, a Type XIV, and *U-504*, a Type IX/C40, were then sunk by Walker's group, and the second Type XIV, *U-461*, by Australian Short Sunderland aircraft.

But whilst the remainder of the operation saw the destruction of 20 U-boats over a nine-week period, 2 SG's time was unproductive, and no further successes were recorded.

Atlantic operations

In September 1943, after a further refit, 2 SG went to the North Atlantic, in company of the escort carrier *Tracker*. The group was joined by *Magpie* (Lt.Cdr R.S. Abrams), while *Woodpecker* was in for repairs.

In October, in concert with B-7 Escort Group, the group worked in support of ON 207. No successes were recorded, though the convoy battle saw three U-boats destroyed, with no ships lost.

However in November 1943, in operations around HX 264, 2 SG accounted for two more U-boats, *U-226* and *U-842*. Whilst the United States Navy had had much success using carrier groups in a hunter killer role on the mid-Atlantic route, the Royal Navy's experience was less positive. Winter gales made flying difficult and hazardous, while the need to provide protection to the carrier hampered A/S operations. 2 SG at least generally had more success operating without carrier assistance.

On December 2 SG was acting in support of SL 140/MKS 31 with 4 SG (Cdr. E.H. Chavasse). 2 SG put in a determined attack on a U-boat, (thought to be *U-843*), but was unsuccessful, though the battle for SL 140/MKS 31 saw the destruction of a U-boat, without loss of ships.

Six in one trip

In January 1944 2 SG sailed on its most famous exploit, accounting for six U-boats in one patrol, three of them in one 15-hour period.

On 31 January 1944 Walker's group gained their first kill of the year when they sank *U-592*. On 9 February his group sank *U-762*, *U-238*, and *U-734* in one action, then sank *U-424* on 11 February, and *U-264* on 19 February. This patrol was ended on 20 February 1944, when one of Walker's group, *Woodpecker*, was torpedoed (possibly by *U-764* or by *U-256*). After an 8-day struggle to get her home, *Woodpecker* sank in a gale off the Scillies; all of her crew were saved. *Woodpecker* was the only ship of 2 SG lost in action.

The group returned to its base at Liverpool to the thrilled jubilation of the city's inhabitants and the Admiralty. The First Lord of the Admiralty was present to greet Walker and his ships. Walker was promoted to Captain and awarded a second Bar to his DSO.

Arctic convoy

In March 1944 the group returned to North Atlantic, destroying *U-653* on weather patrol, before joining Arctic convoy JW 58. It was joined in this for a short period by *Whimbrel*. 2 SG met and destroyed *U-961* in transit across the "Rosegarden", but had no other success, though three U-boats were destroyed in attacks on JW 58. The return convoy, RA 58, was also attacked but neither side saw any success.

In May 1944, 2 SG responded to an attack on USS *Donnell* by *U-473*. Though starting from 300 miles away Walker, in an inspired piece of work, divined where to search and after a three-day search gained contact. An 18-hour hunt brought *U-473* to the surface, where she was sunk by gunfire.

In June 1944, 2 SG was joined by *Dominica*, *Loch Fada*, and *Loch Killin*, replacements for *Kite* and *Magpie*. That month the group was on search and destroy operations in the South-Western Approaches, as part of "Operation Neptune" - the invasion of Normandy, and was instrumental in preventing any attacks on the invasion fleet. In all fifteen U-boats were destroyed in attempts to attack the invasion fleet. Eight ships were sunk.

On July 2 SG received its heaviest blow when Capt. Walker died suddenly of a cerebral haemorrhage.

Later operations

In July 1944, 2 SG was back in action, led initially by *Dominica* (Cdr. N.A. Duck) and later by *Wild Goose* (Cdr. D.E.G. Wemyss).

The group had one successful patrol during August operating in the Bay of Biscay. Four U-boats, *U-333*, *U-736*, *U-608*, and *U-385* were accounted for while attempting to cross the bay to and from their bases.

The months following this were unfruitful, however, as the U-boat Arm changed its tactics to operate in the shallow inland waters around Britain, using the *schnorkel* to remain submerged for entire patrols. This created a different set of tactical problems, requiring different tactics of the escorts.

Last successes

In 1945 *Loch Fada* and *Loch Killin* were transferred, to be replaced by *Loch Ruthven*, *Tobago*, and *Labuan*.

As 2 SG grappled with the changed nature of the campaign the group saw its last successes. In February 1945 the group destroyed two more U-boats, *U-1018* and *U-327* (some sources say this was *U-1208*).

2 SG was also credited with *U-683*, bringing its score to 23. Wemyss reports the attack, in March 1945, but after a report of another sinking in the same area six months earlier, concluded they were "flogging a dead horse".

However a post-war report of *U-683* missing in the area led to 2 SG being credited with her destruction. More recent analysis has questioned this, and the assessment was changed in 1989. It is now thought that 2 SG's attack was on the wreck of *U-247*, sunk in September 1944.

Despite this, 2nd Support Group was responsible for the confirmed destruction of 22 U-boats during World War II, making it the most successful anti-submarine unit of the entire conflict.
Source (edited): "http://en.wikipedia.org/wiki/2nd_Escort_Group_(Royal_Navy)"

36th Escort Group (Royal Navy)

36th Escort Group was a British formation of the Royal Navy which saw action during the Second World War, principally in the Battle of the Atlantic. The group operated mainly on the Gibraltar and South Atlantic convoy routes, and was involved in several convoy battles, including Convoy HG 76, one of the first Allied victories in the Atlantic campaign.

Formation

36th Escort Group (36 EG) was formed in October 1941 led by HMS *Stork* under the command of Cdr FJ "Johnnie" Walker, destined to become Britains most successful anti-submarine warfare commander.

The group comprised 2 sloops, *Stork* and *Deptford* (Lt Cdr HR White), and 7 corvettes *Convulvulus* (Lt RS Connel), *Gardenia* (Lt Cdr Firth), *Marigold* (Lt J Renwick), *Penstemon* (Lt Cdr J Byron), *Rhodedendron* (Lt Cdr LA Sayers), *Samphire* (Lt Cdr FT Renny) and *Vetch* (Lt Cdr HJ Beverley).

Service history

36 Escort Group's first convoy was HG 70, a group of 24 ships homebound from Gibraltar, in August 1941. This was uneventful, as no attack developed. The groups next few convoys, to Gibraltar and the South Atlantic, were equally uneventful, giving the group time to drill and practice group exercises.

In December 1941 36 EG escorted HG 76 in company with the escort carrier *Audacity* and her destroyer consorts. Over a period of 8 days the escort force destroyed 4 U-boats, 3 of them by 36 EG, for the loss of 2 ships and 2 warships, one of which was carrier *Audacity*. Hailed as a major victory, HG 76 was the first time heavy losses had been inflicted on an attacking U-boat force.

In April 1942 the group accompanied OG 82. With a group reduced to *Stork* and 4 corvettes, (*Convulvulus*, *Gardenia*, *Penstemon* and *Vetch*), 36 EG destroyed one U-boat, *U-252*, with no ships lost.

In June 1942 HG 84, escorted by *Stork* with 3 corvettes (*Convulvulus*, *Gardenia* and *Marigold*) was attacked by the U-boat group *Endrass*. The groups aggressive defence caused damage to 5 U-boats, but no kills, while 5 ships were sunk. The destroyer *Wild Swan*, sent as reinforcement, was also sunk in an air attack.

In June Walker left the group to take command of Liverpool base and 36 EG was disbanded, its vessels being transferred to other groups. During its 13 month history 36 EG had escorted 16 convoys. It saw the loss of 9 ships and 2 warships, for the destruction of 4 U-boats and another 5 damaged. Over 400 ships conveyed by 36 EG arrived safely.

Lists

Ships lost

No members of 36 EG were lost

U-boats destroyed

- *U-131* sunk by *Penstemon*, *Stork*, aircraft and 3 other warships on 17 December 1941
- *U-574* rammed by *Stork* on 19 December 1941
- *U-567* depth-charged by *Deptford*

- *U-252* depth-charged by *Vetch* and *Stork* on 14 April 1942

Source (edited): "http://en.wikipedia.org/wiki/36th_Escort_Group_(Royal_Navy)"

3rd Battle Squadron (United Kingdom)

King Edward VII-class battleships on maneuvers ca. 1909.

The British Royal Navy **3rd Battle Squadron** was a naval squadron consisting of battleships and other vessels, active from at least 1914 to 1945. The 3rd Battle Squadron was initially part of the Royal Navy's Home Fleet. During the First World War, the Home Fleet was renamed the Grand Fleet. During the Second World War, the squadron covered Atlantic convoys.

First World War

On 5 August 1914, the squadron had eight ships: *King Edward VII*, *Africa*, *Britannia*, *Commonwealth*, *Dominion*, *Hibernia*, *Hindustan* and *New Zealand*. The squadron of eight *King Edward VII*-class pre-dreadnought battleships were nicknamed "the wobbly eight" after their slight tendency to roll under way.

The squadron was initially used as part of the Grand Fleet in support of the cruisers on the Northern Patrol. On 29 April 1916, the 3rd Battle Squadron was moved to Sheerness from Rosyth and came under the Nore Command in the Thames estuary. The move was intended to make more large ships available for coastal defence duties, after the Bombardment of Yarmouth and Lowestoft by German ships on 24 April 1916.

Essentially made obsolete by the introduction of the revolutionary battleship *Dreadnought*, and as battleships the world over began mimicking her design, the 3rd Battle Squadron played no role in the Battle of Jutland. The need for accompanying destroyers for these battleships was later given as the reason the Harwich destroyer squadron was also held back and took no part in the Jutland action.

Following the loss of *King Edward VII* in January 1916, *Africa* and *Britannia* served in the Mediterranean 1916-1917. The remaining ships were augmented by *Dreadnought* until March 1918.

Second World War

At the start of the Second World War, the squadron formed part of the Channel Force and comprised just two ships:
- *Resolution* - flagship of Rear Admiral L. E. Holland; Captain C. H. Knox Little;
- *Revenge* - Captain E. R. Archer.

Later in the war, the squadron was based at Halifax, Nova Scotia. Rear Admiral, Third Battle Squadron, was responsible for covering Atlantic convoys. RMS *Ascania*—an armed merchant cruiser—was part of the squadron during this period. *Seaborn*—a Fleet Air Arm base was established at RCAF Station Dartmouth in September 1940. *Seaborn* was to provide a shore base with administrative and maintenancd facilities for the Swordfish and Walrus aircraft assigned to ships of the Third Battle Squadron.

In 1942, the Third Battle Squadron, now comprising;
- *Resolution* - flagship of Vice Admiral W. E. C. Tait; Captain A. R. Halfhide;
- *Ramillies* - Captain D. N. C. Tuffnell;
- *Revenge* - Captain L. V. Morgan;
- *Royal Sovereign* Captain R. H. Portal; sailed for the Far East and became was part of the Eastern Fleet. The squadron formed part of Force B. Facing the superior striking force of the Japanese *Kido Butai* carrier striking force during the 1941 Indian Ocean raid, the slow component of the Eastern Fleet—including the battleships of Force B—was withdrawn all the way back to Kilindini in East Africa to avoid their destruction at Japanese hands. *Hermes*—Force B's sole aircraft carrier—was detached and destroyed near Ceylon.

In 1945, the Squadron consisted of two battleships, *Queen Elizabeth* and the Free French *Richelieu*, as well another two escort carriers, four cruisers and six destroyers. Two battleships and escort carriers formed part of the covering force for Operation Dracula, the retaking of Rangoon. Vice-Admiral H.T.C. Walker commanded the squadron at the time.

Source (edited): "http://en.wikipedia.org/wiki/3rd_Battle_Squadron_(United_Kingdom)"

5th Escort Group (Royal Navy)

5th Escort Group was a British formation of the Royal Navy which saw action during the Second World War, principally in the Battle of the Atlantic.

Formation

5th Escort Group (5 EG) was formed in March 1941, one of the earliest escort groups to be set up. Led by Cdr Donald MacIntyre as Senior Officer Escort (SOE) in HMS *Walker*, 5 EG comprised the V class destroyers *Vanoc*, and *Volunteer*, the S-class destroyers *Sardonyx* and *Scimitar* and the Flower class corvettes *Bluebell* and *Hydrangea*

Service history

5 EG's first action was a major convoy battle in defence of HX 112 in March 1941. This saw the loss of 5 ships but also the destruction of 2 U-boats *U-99* and *U-100*, commanded by leading U-boat aces Kretschmer and Schepke.

5 EG continued on escort duty in the North Atlantic but this became uneventful due to a downturn in the U-boat effectiveness in Summer of 1941. This was due to the loss of three U-boat aces in March, and British Intelligence penetration of the U-boat Arms Enigma code after April.

In June 5 EG moved to escort south- and north-bound convoys to and from Gibraltar and the South Atlantic. These too were successful, despite the threat across the Bay of Biscay of both air and U-boat attack.

In October 1941 5 EG returned to escort duty in the North Atlantic.

The group underwent several changes, as ships were transferred, or were docked for extended repair. In December 1941 Macintyre was posted to Argentia as liaison officer, and, as and as all the ships had become worn out, 5 EG was disbanded after 9 months service.

During this period 5 EG had escorted over two dozen convoys, totalling over 700 ships of which just 12 were lost. No warships were lost from the group, which accounted for 2 U-boats in its career.

Source (edited): "http://en.wikipedia.org/wiki/5th_Escort_Group_(Royal_Navy)"

700 Naval Air Squadron

700 Naval Air Squadron (700 NAS) is a squadron of aircraft in the Royal Navy's Fleet Air Arm.

History

700 NAS was originally formed in January 1940 at RNAS Hatston (HMS *Sparrowhawk*) in Orkney in a plan to centralise the operations of the 700 series "Catapult" flights attached to catapult units and to act a pool and Headquarters for all catapult aircraft embarked on battleships and cruisers - chiefly the Supermarine Walrus flying boat and Fairey Seafox floatplane.

On 21 June 1940, a Walrus (*P5666*) of 700 Squadron on the cruiser HMS *Manchester* found the German battleship *Scharnhorst* but HMS *Manchester* did not engage.

Trailing German capital ships in the lead up to the Battle of the Denmark Strait, Walrus *L2184* of 700 NAS from HMS *Norfolk* was damaged by shellfire from *Prinz Eugen* in the Denmark Strait on 23 May 1941 while still on its catapult.

The final successful attack on an enemy submarine by a Walrus was on 11 July 1942, when Walrus *W2709* of 700 (Levant) NAS sank the Italian submarine *Ondina*, along with the surface vessels South African *Protea* and trawler *Southern Maid*, east of Cyprus.

There were at least 5 confirmed enemy submarines sunk or damaged by Walruses during the Second World War, including the Vichy French submarine *Poncelet* which was bombed by Walrus *L2268* of 700 NAS (HMS *Devonshire*) and attacked by HMS *Milford* on 7 November 1940 off the Cameroons. The submarine was damaged and forced to surrender, and later scuttled off the Gulf of Guinea. The crew of Petty Officer P H Parsons, Sub Lt A D Corkhill and N A Evans were all awarded gallantry medals.

700 NAS was disbanded in March 1944, pilots transferring into 771 Naval Air Squadron, but it was reformed as a Test Pilot School in October 1944.

700 NAS re-emerged in August 1955 as a Fleet Requirements unit and from 1957 was based out of RNAS Lee-on-Solent to introduce the Whirlwind HAS. 7.

The Squadron carried on trials of de Havilland Sea Vixens on HMS *Victorious* and HMS *Centaur* during 1958 and from October 1959 formed at Yeovilton with the Saunders Roe P.531 to investigate what would be needed to introduce a whole new form of helicopter operation to the Fleet – which lead to the Westland Wasp.

In October 1960 flight tests of landing and take-offs from HMS *Vengeance* with 27 launchings of the turboprop Fairey Gannet and 34 with the Hawker Sea Hawk.

A 700Z Sqn Buccaneer S.1 at RNAS Lossiemouth in 1961.

700 NAS disbanded again at RNAS Yeovilton in July 1961. However, a number of Intensive Flying Trials Units were subsequently formed under the "700 NAS" title, to prepare for new aircraft types coming into service. These operated as independent units, each being identified by a suffix letter after the squadron number (eg. "700B").

Several of these IFTUs were formed for the introduction of the Westland Wessex, Blackburn Buccaneer, McDonnell Douglas Phantom, Westland Sea King, Westland Lynx and BAe Sea Harrier into the Fleet Air Arm.

More recently, the squadron was re-commissioned at RNAS Culdrose in December 1998 as 700M Squadron, with a primary role of testing and evaluating the Merlin HM.1 helicopter. 700M disbanded on 31 March 2008, transferring its aircraft and personnel to 824 Naval Air Squadron and also forming a new flight, 824 OEU. The squadron reformed again as 700W NAS in May 2009 at Yeovilton as the Lynx Wildcat Fielding Squadron. 700W expects to receive up to five Wildcats from January 2013 for operational evaluation and conversion training.

Aircraft operated

- AgustaWestland Merlin
- Westland Lynx (introduction to service)
- Supermarine Walrus
- Westland Whirlwind (tests)
- De Havilland Sea Vixen
- Fairey Gannet (tests)
- Hawker Sea Hawk (tests)
- Saunders-Roe P.531 (tests) (only 6 built)
- Westland Wasp (introduction to service)
- Westland Sea King (introduction to service)

Source (edited): "http://en.wikipedia.org/wiki/700_Naval_Air_Squadron"

750 Naval Air Squadron

"Royal Navy Observer School" redirects here

The **Royal Navy Observer School** grew out of HM Naval Seaplane Training School at RNAS Lee-on-Solent as a result of a series of changes of identity and parent unit. From 1918 until 1939 the Royal Air Force was responsible for naval aviation, including training and provision of aircrew to the Royal Navy. With the return of naval aviation to the Royal Navy on 24 May 1939, the Observer School was established as **750 Naval Air Squadron** of the Fleet Air Arm. During World War II the squadron moved to Trinidad to continue training aircrew. It was temporarilly disbanded in October 1945. The squadron reformed in 1952 and is currently based at RNAS Culdrose, where it trains approximately 30 Royal Navy observers every year.

History

The Royal Navy established **HM Naval Seaplane Training School** on 30 July 1917 at Lee-on-Solent; the unit was responsible for the training of seaplane pilots and observers. When the Royal Naval Air Service and the Royal Flying Corps merged on 1 April 1918 to form the Royal Air Force, the school was renamed **No. 209 Training Depot**.

Fairey IIID

Throughout the early 1920s pilots and observers of seaplanes were trained at Lee-on-Solent under a variety of names; from 1921 the base was renamed the **RAF Seaplane Training School**, and from 1923, the **RAF School of Naval Co-operation**. Although the school now concentrated on observer training, from 1925 all naval aircrew were provided by the RAF, and training of naval officers as observers ceased. During this period the primary training aircraft was the Fairey IIID.

From 1932 Lee-on-Solent was provided with a full airfield and became the headquarters of the RAF's Coastal Command. Observer training continued apace and the airfield was home to a wide range of naval aircraft including Fairey Seals, Hawker Ospreys, Blackburn Sharks, Supermarine Walruses, and Fairey Swordfishes. Telegraphist Air Gunners were also trained at Lee-on-Solent in the years leading up to the Second World War.

Fairey Barracuda II

750 Naval Air Squadron was formed at RNAS Ford on 24 May 1939 from the Royal Navy Observer School, but after Ford was bombed early in the war, it moved to RNAS Yeovilton. Changing title from a school to a squadron did not change its basic purpose, which was the training of observers for the Fleet Air Arm. The squadron initially flew Hawker Ospreys and Blackburn Sharks, but in November 1940 it moved to Piarco Savannah (HMS *Goshawk*) in Trinidad and at about the same time re-equipped with Fairey Albacores.

The squadron operated in Trinidad for the duration of World War II and was disbanded on 10 October 1945. The squadron reformed on 17 April 1952 at RNAS St Merryn. At first it was equipped with twelve Fairey Barracudas and four Avro Ansons, but in 1953 the Fairey Firefly T7 and Percival Sea Prince T1 aircraft were introduced, and in the same year the squadron moved to RNAS Culdrose. In 1955 the squadron changed its name to the **Observer and Air Signal School**. After discontinuing the training of air telegraphists, it changed again to the **Observer School** in May 1959.

The squadron moved to Hal Far (HMS *Falcon*), Malta in October 1959, and in 1965 it was transferred again, this time to RNAS Lossiemouth. The last move came in 1972, back to RNAS Culdrose, and at the same time the squadron was re-equipped with the Handley Page Jetstream T1. The more modern T2 version of the Jetstream arrived in 1978 and in 1992 the squadron became the first Naval Air Squadron to achieve 50 unbroken years in commission.

Current role

Jetstream T2 XX481 of 750 NAS landing at RNAS Culdrose

Now flying the T2 & T3 versions of the BAe Jetstream, 750 NAS is tasked with training the Fleet Air Arm's Observers. After undergoing initial training at Britannia Royal Naval College, trainee aircrew officers join 750 NAS for a seven-month period of training in all aspects of airborne navigation, airmanship and other tactical skills. This is conducted in classrooms as well as in the air and in a computer-controlled simulator. Upon completion of this course they will be ready for Advanced Flying Training and will be streamed for their eventual specialisation.

On completion of the training observers choose or are selected to serve in Westland Sea King, Westland Lynx or AugustaWestland Merlin helicopters. These then help extend the eyes and ears of the fleet at sea.

In 2011, the Jetstreams were replaced by Beechcraft Super King Air 350ER (Avenger) aircraft.

Aircraft flown

Since 1939 705 NAS has flown 13 types of aircraft:

Blackburn Shark

- Blackburn Shark II
- Fairey Albacore I
- Fairey Barracuda II & TR3
- North American Harvard
- Avro Anson I
- Percival Sea Prince T1
- Fairey Firefly T7
- Airspeed Oxford I
- de Havilland Sea Vampire T22
- de Havilland Sea Venom FAW21 & FAW22
- de Havilland Sea Devon C20
- Handley Page (later BAe) Jetstream T1, T2 & T3
- Beechcraft Super King Air 350ER

Source (edited): "http://en.wikipedia.org/wiki/750_Naval_Air_Squadron"

792 Naval Air Squadron

792 Naval Air Squadron of the Fleet Air Arm of the Royal Navy was originally formed at St. Merryn in August 1939 as an Air Target Unit, equipped with six Blackburn Skuas. The squadron disbanded in 1945 and merged with 794 Squadron.

792 Squadron reformed at RNAS Culdrose in 1948 as a Night Fighter Training Unit. It was initially equipped with Firefly NF.1s and Avro Ansons. They were later replaced with Sea Hornets shortly before the squadron disbanded again in August 1950.

The squadron was reformed at RNAS Culdrose in November 2001 from the Fleet Target Group from RNAS Portland, which closed in 1998. It operates the Mirach 100/5 unmanned subsonic drones which are used to test the Sea Dart Missile System on Type 42 Destroyers and Sidewinder missiles on Harrier and Tornado fighters.

Source (edited): "http://en.wikipedia.org/wiki/792_Naval_Air_Squadron"

835 Naval Air Squadron

835 Naval Air Squadron was a squadron of the Royal Navy's Fleet Air Arm formed originally as a Fairey Swordfish torpedo bomber/reconnaissance unit in February 1942. In June 1943, six Sea Hurricanes were added to the squadron as a fighter flight. The composite unit exchanged these in September 1944 for Grumman Wildcats, serving on until 1 April 1945, when the squadron disbanded.

History

1942

HMS *Furious* at sea, circa 1935-36, with a flight of Blackburn Baffin torpedo planes overhead.

The history of the squadron begins in Eastleigh near Southampton in Hampshire. There, in January 1942, the first members of the squadron assembled at the Royal Naval Air Station (RNAS) Eastleigh, also known as HMS Raven. On 29 January they left for Glasgow to board the SS Andalucia Star, which brought them to Jamaica, leaving Glasgow on 4 February and arriving in Kinston on 17 February. 835 Naval Air Squadron officially forming that day at Palisadoes (HMS Buzzard), Jamaica as a torpedo-bomber/reconnaissance Fairey Swordfish squadron. They left Jamaica 12 March 1942, having done some patrols over the seas around Jamaica, going to Norfolk, Virginia, USA where a refitted HMS *Furious* lay waiting for them to take them aboard They left Norfolk on 3 April 1942 for the UK, arriving 15 April at RNAS Lee-on-Solent (HMS Daedalus), Hampshire. In June 1942 they moved to RNAS Hatston (HMS Sparrowhawk), Orkney, Scotland. It was a time of continuous relocation and 22 September 1942 they moved further to RNAS Stretton (HMS Blackcap), Cheshire, moving on 29 October to RNAS Machrihanish (HMS Landrail), Argyll. November 1942 was spent doing initial Deck Launch Training (DLT) on HMS *Activity*. and December saw a return to RNAS Machrihanish and a further relocation to RAF Kirkistown, County Down, Northern Ireland, where they stayed till 29 January 1943.

1943

HMS *Battler* underway.

On 29 January, they moved back to RNAS Machrihanish (earning the nickname "Clapham Junction" with the squadron), but the next move was finally to a carrier: the squadron embarked on HMS *Battler* on 8 April 1943 for convoy duties, but they had to leave on 7 May, returning to RNAS Machrihanish for RP-3 Rocker Projectile training. After a short return to the Battler, followed a move on 15 May to RAF Ballykelly, County Londonderry, Northern Ireland and a further one on 22 May to RNAS Eglington (HMS Gannet). In June 1943, a flight of six Sea Hurricane Mk.IIcs from 804 squadron joined the squadron, which spent part of September and October of 1943 operating from HMS *Ravager*, while part of the Swordfishes served on HMS *Argus* and the rest of the squadron remained at RAF Ayr, Ayrshire, Scotland. After a period ashore at RNAS Eglington, the squadron shortly embarked on HMS *Chaser*, only to be taken off three weeks later and being transferred to RNAS Abbotsinch (HMS Sanderling) and later again to RNAS Eglington.

1944

British escort carrier HMS *Nairana* underway.

On 31 December 1943, the squadron transferred to the escort carrier HMS *Nairana*, returning ashore at RNAS Hatston and RNAS Machrihanish (HMS Landrail) in January 1944. Most of 1944, however, was spent onboard *Nairana*, on Atlantic convoy duties and on the Gibraltar Run. The squadron also served in 1944 with a successful submarine Hunter-Killer Group in the North Atlantic under the overall command of Captain Frederick Walker. In May-June 1944, three Ju 290s were shot down. In August 1944, the squadron became involved in the Murmansk Convoys to and from RNAS Hatston, where it faced the most dangerous flying conditions of the war, and attacked two U-Boats and shot down four enemy aircraft. September 1944 saw the arrival of the Grumman Wildcat Mk.VIs, replacing the by now aging Sea Hurricanes.

1945

An example of a still-flying Fairey Swordfish.

On 9 January 1945, Lt-Commander John Godley RNVR—who had previously been in command of 'P' Flight of 836 Naval Air Squadron—became commander of the squadron. Before that, the squadron was led by Lieutenant-Commander Val Jones, a Swordfish Observer. The Senior Pilot of the squadron was Lieutenant Allen Burgham, DSC, MiD, who flew Sea Hurricane Mk.IIcs and later Wildcat Mk.VIs, and was Flight Commander of the Fighter Component. At this time, the squadron was flying 14 Swordfish and six Grumman Wildcat aircraft.

Lieutenant-Commander John Godley served as Squadron Commanding Officer for one Murmansk Convoy in February 1945. 835 Squadron saw further combat doing two coastal anti-shipping raids along the Norwegian coast off Trondheim, before being disbanded on 1 April 1945 at RNAS Hatston, with its fighter flight transferring to 821 Naval Air Squadron. Lt/Cdr. Godley was transferred to command 714 Naval Air Squadron.

Aircraft operated

an example of a still flying Hawker Sea Huricane

Source (edited): "http://en.wikipedia.org/wiki/835_Naval_Air_Squadron"

Allied Technical Air Intelligence Unit

The **Allied Technical Air Intelligence Unit** (ATAIU) was a joint group of the United States Navy, United States Army Air Forces, Royal Australian Air Force, and Royal Navy formed in November 1942 to recover Japanese aircraft to obtain intelligence on their technical and tactical capabilities. Crashed and captured aircraft were located, identified, and evaluated (often in or near the front lines), before being recovered for further tests. Aircraft that were not too badly damaged were rebuilt for test flights that revealed vulnerabilities that could be exploited. Examination of the materials used in the construction of aircraft allowed the Allies to analyse Japanese war production. The unit also absorbed a small team who developed the code name system for Japanese aircraft, and produced aircraft recognition charts and photographs.

Early technical air intelligence operations

The attack on Pearl Harbor demonstrated the key role of aircraft in the Pacific War, but the United States possessed virtually no information about the capabilities of Japanese aircraft. Several shot down aircraft were recovered from Hawaii and examined by the U.S. Navy and USAAF, who completed their own separate studies. The USAAF formed a unit based at Wright Field, Ohio, with the assistance of the British Royal Air Force's technical intelligence section, which had been operating successfully since 1939. Meanwhile, the U.S. Navy set up a captured enemy equipment unit at Naval Air Station Anacostia outside Washington D.C. A joint Army-Navy Technical Air Intelligence Unit was proposed, but neither service was prepared to work with the other.

The British and Australians carried out most of the field technical intelligence operations during early months of the war. The battlefields of Papua New Guinea yielded the first examples of enemy aircraft. Several wrecks were recovered around Port Moresby, and in early 1942 a Japanese Mitsubishi A6M Zero was discovered nearly intact and shipped to Australia for examination. In June 1942 another "Zero" made a forced landing at Akutan in the Aleutian Islands. The aircraft was recovered by the U.S. Navy and shipped to NAS North Island, California, where it was repaired and made a number of test flights to determine its performance and capabilities.

ATAIU operations

It was in order to consolidate and co-ordinate these different operations that the Allied Technical Air Intelligence Unit was formed, based in Hangar 7 at the RAAF/USAAF Eagle Farm Airbase outside Brisbane, Australia, in November 1942.

The ATAIU's first success came after the Battle of Buna–Gona in early 1943. The first examples of the Mitsubishi A6M3 "Hamp" were captured largely intact at Buna Airfield. Several other aircraft, engines and other components were sent to Eagle Farm, and in early 1943 an "Zero" was built using parts from five different aircraft. Test flights included a mock dogfight against a Spitfire V. It was concluded that the "Zero" was superior to the Spitfire below 20,000 feet. In late 1943 the aircraft was shipped to the United States aboard the escort carrier *Copahee*, and sent to Wright Field where it was flown and evaluated.

Further success came in late December 1943, when U.S. Marines captured the airfield at Cape Gloucester on the north coast of New Britain, finding many wrecks and several nearly intact aircraft. ATAIU officers logged the serial numbers of the aircraft, and engine configurations, serial numbers and dates of manufacture. They inspected cockpits for layout and control locations, and armour plate. They recovered armaments and noted their locations and mounts. Some reports provided considerable detail, including oil and fuel tank capacities, and special electronics installed. One of these was a Kawasaki Ki-45 "Nick" fighter, about which little was known. Another fighter, a Kawasaki Ki-61 "Tony", was also examined.

Mitsubishi A6M2 "Zero" at the National Museum of the United States Air Force at Dayton, Ohio. This aircraft was found near Kavieng on New Ireland, Papua New Guinea, and probably operated by the 6th *Kokutai* (Squadron) and later by the 253rd *Kokutai*. It is painted to represent a section leader's aircraft from the aircraft carrier *Zuihō* during the Battle of the Bismarck Sea in March 1943.

One of the biggest problems faced by the ATAIU teams was Allied troops, who commonly stripped enemy aircraft for "souvenirs". Efforts were made to minimize indiscriminate souvenir hunting and troops were encouraged to turn in all captured items and report enemy aircraft wrecks. Most of these efforts were in vain, and it remained a constant problem throughout the war. Another obstacle was that most Japanese aircraft fell into the ocean, and those that did not often crashed in isolated areas that were difficult to reach. As an example, a newly-developed Yokosuka D4Y "Judy" dive bomber with an in-line engine crashed six miles inland, on a 1,500-foot (460 m) hill, on Santa Isabel Island. The ATAIU had to recruit local men to cut a trail to the crash site with machetes, and then carry out the engine on a cradle woven from tree bark.

Crashed Enemy Aircraft Reports (CEARs) were systematically compiled from April 1943. In February 1944, it was agreed that production data on enemy equipment was essential, and more extensive reports detailed the age and condition of captured equipment to give an indication of the general state of the Japanese war economy, paying particular attention to the name plates and markings which gave information on the manufacturers. Eventually a special unit known as "JAPLATE" was created to conduct this task, and 6,336 intact name plates or their details were collected.

In mid-1944, U.S. Navy personnel were withdrawn from the ATAIU and reassigned to NAS Anacosta to form the Technical Air Intelligence Centre (TAIC) to centralise and co-ordinate the work of test centres in the United States with the work of TAIUs in the field. The unit was then renamed **TAIU for the South West Pacific Area** (TAIU-SWPA).

Technical Air Intelligence operations were fully developed by the time of the invasion of the Philippines. Considerable instruction was given to the troops on the equipment likely to be found and the importance of its preservation. The TAIU-SWPA moved from Australia to the Philippines in early 1945 and gained an appreciation of the state of enemy technological and economic development essential to the build-up for the planned invasion of Japan. Aircraft acquired there included examples of the Mitsubishi A6M Zero, Mitsubishi J2M "Jack", Kawasaki Ki-45 "Nick", Kawasaki Ki-61 "Tony", Kawanishi N1K "George", Nakajima Ki-44 "Tojo", and Nakajima Ki-84 "Frank" fighters; the Nakajima B5N "Kate", Nakajima B6N "Jill", Yokosuka D4Y "Judy", and Mitsubishi G4M "Betty" bombers; the Showa L2D "Tabby" transport, and the Mitsubishi Ki-46 "Dinah" reconnaissance aircraft.

Other Technical Air Intelligence Units

A joint RAF/USAAF unit, known as the "ATAIU for South East Asia" (ATAIU-SEA) was formed in Calcutta in late 1943, and disbanded at Singapore in 1946. Two other units were also created; "TAIU for the Pacific Ocean Area" (TAIU-POA), a U.S. Navy unit which operated in the Pacific Islands, and "TAIU for China" (TAIU-CHINA) under the control of Chiang Kai-shek's Nationalists.

Post-war operations

Technical Air Intelligence Units operated in Japan after the end of the war, shifting from tactical intelligence to post-hostilities investigations. General Hap Arnold ordered the preservation of four of every type of aircraft one of each for the USAAF, USN, RAF and museum collections. By the end of 1945 these were collected together at Yokohama Naval Base. One hundred and fifteen aircraft were shipped to the United States, with 73 going to the Army and 42 to the Navy. However, lack of funds, storage space and interest meant that only six aircraft were restored, flown and evaluated by the Army and only two by the Navy. Eventually, 46 complete aircraft were sent to various museums while the rest were scrapped. By early 1946 ATAIU-SEA in Singapore had collected 64 Japanese Army and Navy aircraft, most in flyable condition, for shipment to the UK. However lack of shipping space prevented this operation and only four eventually arrived in England to be put in display in museums.

Source (edited): "http://en.wikipedia.org/wiki/Allied_Technical_Air_Intelligence_Unit"

B-2 Escort Group (Royal Navy)

B-2 Escort Group was a British formation of the Royal Navy which saw action during the Second World War, principally in the Battle of the Atlantic. The group was under the command of Cdr Donald Macintyre, one of Britains most successful anti-submarine warfare commanders.

Formation

B-2 Escort Group (B-2 EG) was one of seven British escort groups which served with the Mid-Ocean Escort

Force (MOEF), which provided convoy protection in the most dangerous mid-section of the North Atlantic route.

B-2 EG was formed in the spring of 1942 and originally consisted of the Havant class destroyer HMS Hesperus with Town class destroyer *Leamington*, V and W class destroyer *Veteran*, and Flower-class corvettes HMS Gentian (K90), HMS Clematis, *Sweetbriar* and *Vervain*.

Later in the year the low-endurance destroyers *Leamington* and *Veteran* were replaced by long-range V&W destroyers *Vanessa* and *Whitehall* and corvettes HMS Heather, HMS Campanula, and HMS Mignonette joined the group.

Service history

B-2 EG commenced convoy escort duties in April 1942, in the critical mid ocean section of the North Atlantic route, operating between RN Londonderry and St Johns Newfoundland.

The spring and early summer B-2's first convoys, in the spring of 1942, were uneventful, and as the pace of the Battle of the Atlantic hotted up in the summer and autumn the group's convoys were escorted without loss.

In October 1942, ON 138 came under attack, but a vigorous defence by B-2 ensured no ships were lost. In December 1942, accompanying HX 219 the convoy came under attack. *Hesperus* responded and counter-attacked and destroyed *U-357* by ramming. As a result *Hesperus* was out of action for 2 months.

In February 1943 a depleted B-2 under temporary command of Cdr Proudfoot escorted Convoy SC 118. This convoy came under attack by wolfpack *Pfeil* and lost 8 ships for 3 U-boats destroyed in one of the hardest fought battles of the campaign.

In April during an attack on ONS 4, B-2 ships sank *U-191*.

In May in an attack on SC 129 B-2 sank *U-186* and damaged *U-402* and *U-223* for the loss of 2 ships.

A series of uneventful convoys followed, as the U-boat Arm withdrew from the North Atlantic after Black May, a state of affairs which continued until the end of the year

During this period B-2 EG had escorted over 30 convoys, totalling over 900 ships of which just 10 were lost. No warships were lost from the group, which accounted for 3 U-boats destroyed and 2 others damaged, and shared in the destruction of 3 others, in its 2 year career.

Lists

Ships lost

No members of B-2 EG were lost

U-boats destroyed

- *U-357*, sunk by *Hesperus* and *Vanessa* on 26 December 1942
- *U-191*, sunk by *Hesperus* on 23 April 1943
- *U-186* sunk by *Hesperus* on 12 May 1943

Source (edited): "http://en.wikipedia.org/wiki/B-2_Escort_Group_(Royal_Navy)"

B-6 Escort Group (Royal Navy)

B-6 Escort Group was a British formation of the Royal Navy which saw action during the Second World War, principally in the Battle of the Atlantic.

Formation

B-6 Escort Group (B-6 EG)was one of seven British escort groups which served with the Mid-Ocean Escort Force (MOEF), which provided convoy protection in the most dangerous mid-section of the North Atlantic route. The MOEF was originally to be 5 American, 5 British and 4 Canadian groups. B-6 was formed in the spring of 1942, following the inability of the USN to form groups A-4 and A-5 due to other commitments. To replace them two new escort groups, B-6 and B-7 were formed.

Service history

Led by V&W class destroyer *Viscount*, and under the leadership of Cdr JJ Waterhouse, B-6 comprised 4 Norwegian-manned corvettes from A-4; *Acanthus*, *Eglantine*, *Potentilla*, and *Rose*. These were joined later by a fifth, *Monbretia*.

In the summer of 1942 B-6 escorted several uneventful convoys which arrived without loss. However in August 1942 ON 122 was attacked by 9 U-boats of wolfpack *Lohs* . 4 ships were sunk, while 6 U-boats were damaged , 4 seriously enough to return to base. Two of these later attacked on their return by aircraft in the Bay of Biscay; one was sunk, another so badly damaged it had to be withdrawn from service..

In September B-6 was joined by the destroyer *Fame* as senior ship, whose commander R Heathcote became Senior Officer of the Escort group (SOE).

In October SC 104 was attacked by Group *Wotan* In a 5 day battle (12-17 Oct) SC 104 lost 8 ships while 2 U boats (*U-661* and *U-353*) were destroyed and 2 others damaged. During this action both *Fame* and *Viscount* were damaged and forced to withdraw, command falling on Cdr CA Momsen of *Potentilla* .

In November a depleted B-6 group, still under Momsen, was escorting ON 144 which was attacked by 16 U boats of Group *Kreuzotter*. In a fierce battle, 5 ships of the convoy, and the corvette *Monbretia*, were sunk. One U-boat was destroyed (*U-184*, sunk by *Potentilla*). Monsen and the group were later commended for their aggressive defence, which was widely held to have averted a major disaster.

In December HX 217 was attacked by 7 U-boats of group *Panzer*. B-6, again led by *Fame*, and with the 3 Norwegians was now joined by Polish destroyer *Burza*, and a British corvette. *Another aggressive defence kept losses to a minimum, even when* Panzer *was joined by a second wolf pack, Draufgang. 2 ships were sunk in the 3 day battle, while one U boat was sunk by aircraft, and several others damaged. Another U boat was lost, and one damaged, in a mid-ocean collision*

In Jan 43 B-6 was joined by the corvettes *Kingcup* and *Vervain*, bringing its strength up to 7 warships.

In February 1943 while escorting ON 165, the convoy was attacked by U-boats of Group *Hardegen*. Two U-boats were destroyed in this assault, (*U-69* sunk by *Fame* and *U-201* by *Viscount*) for the loss of 2 ships .

In late February and early March HX 227 was intercepted by group *Neptun*, but an aggressive defence and foul weather frustrated any co-ordinated attacks. 2 straggler were lost, while 2 U-boats were forced to return with damage.

Following the major convoy battles of May 1943, which left B-6 and their charges unscathed, the Battle of the Atlantic fell into a lull as the U-boat Arm withdrew from the battle. Several uneventful convoys followed, until the renewal of the offensive in the autumn of 1943.

In this period B-6 was involved in one convoy battle, while escorting ON 206. This convoy, and ONS 20, both became embroiled in the last major convoy action of the campaign, which saw 6 U-boats destroyed, for one ships lost. None of these were accounted to ships of B-6 however.

Following this action the North Atlantic route was again quiet, with B-6 continuing escort duties, until in the spring of 1944 it was disbanded in a general re-organization prior to the invasion of Normandy.

In its 23 month career B-6 escorted 31 convoys, losing 19 ships, but seeing over 900 safely to harbour. The group lost one of its number, the corvette *Monbretia*, but was credited with the destruction of five U-boats.

Tables

Ships lost

- *Monbretia*, torpedoed and sunk 18 November 1942 by *U-262*

U-Boats destroyed

- *U-661* rammed by *Viscount* on 15 October 1942
- *U-353* rammed by *Fame* on 16 October 1942
- *U-184* depth-charged by *Potentilla* on 20 November 1942
- *U-69* rammed by *Viscount* on 17 February 1943
- *U-201* depth-charged by *Fame* on 17 February 1943

Source (edited): "http://en.wikipedia.org/wiki/B-6_Escort_Group_(Royal_Navy)"

B-7 Escort Group (Royal Navy)

B-7 Escort Group was a British formation of the Royal Navy which saw action during the Second World War, principally in the Battle of the Atlantic.

Formation

B-7 Escort Group (B-7 EG) was one of seven British escort groups which served with the Mid-Ocean Escort Force (MOEF), which provided convoy protection in the most dangerous mid-section of the North Atlantic route. The MOEF was originally to be 5 American, 5 British and 4 Canadian groups. B-7 was formed in the spring of 1942, following the inability of the USN to form groups A-4 and A-5 due to other commitments. To replace them two new escort groups, B-6 and B-7 were formed.

Service history

B-7 Group Leader HMS *Firedrake*

Led by *Firedrake*, and under the leadership of Cdr WE Banks, B-7 comprised six Flower class corvette; *Loosestrife* from the disbanded American group A-5, and *Alisma, Coreopsis, Jonquil, Pink* and *Sunflower*. These were joined later by the destroyers *Chesterfield* and *Ripley*

B-7's first convoys, in the spring of 1942, were uneventful, and as the pace of the Battle of the Atlantic hotted up in the summer and autumn the group's convoys were escorted without loss. But in December 1942, while escorting ON 153 the convoy came under attack, and 3 ships were sunk. During this action, on 11 December, *Firedrake* was torpedoed by *U-211* and sank with the loss of 168 of her crew, including her current commander, and group SOE, Cdr EH Tilden.

B-7s new SOE assigned was Cdr PW Gretton, of *Duncan*, a tough and capable leader, who quickly moulded B-7 to his own image.

B-7 Group Leader HMS *Duncan*

At this point B-7 comprised the destroyers *Duncan, Vidette*, the frigate *Tay*, and the corvettes *Alisma, Loosestrife, Pink, Sunflower* and *Snowflake*.

After several convoys escorted without loss, B-7 escorted HX 231 in April 1943. This came under attack by the

Lowenherz U-boat group, which sank 6 ships, but lost 2 U-boats destroyed, and 5 damaged. In May 1943 B-7 escorted ONS 5, sometimes regarded as the turning point of the Atlantic campaign. In a week long battle against 3 U-boat groups, *Star*, *Amstel* and later *Fink*, ONS 5 saw the loss of 13 ships, for the destruction of 6 U-boats. At least 4 of these were credited to ships of B-7 EG. Later in May returning with SC 130, B-7 saw the destruction of between 3 and 5 U-boats (sources vary) for no losses. at least one of these was credited to ships of B-7 EG.

A series of uneventful convoys followed, as the U-boat Arm withdrew from the North Atlantic after Black May, while Gretton lobbied for a chance for B-7 to operate as a Support Group.

In October 1943 this was given, as the U-boat Arm launched its autumn offensive. B-7 was involved in the battles for convoys ONS 20 and ON 206, ON 207 and ON 208, during which period 9 U-boats were destroyed. The battle for ONS20/206 saw 6 U-boats destroyed, of which *U-631* was credited to *Sunflower* and another, *U-844* was damaged by *Duncan*, to be destroyed later in an air attack. ON 207 saw 3 U-boats destroyed, one (*U-282*) by ships of B-7, and another shared with aircraft. During this period B-7 had steamed 6,700 miles, crossing back and forth across the Atlantic five times. The group members had refueled at sea on six occasions, and had also re-armed with depth charges at sea.

Following this B-7 returned to escort duty on the North Atlantic route, continuing without major incident until the group was disbanded in the summer of 1944 as part of the preparations for Operation Neptune.

Lists

Ships lost

- HMS *Firedrake* torpedoed and sunk by *U-211* escorting convoy ON 153 on 11 December 1942.

U-Boats destroyed

- *U-192* depth-charged by *Pink* on 5 May 1943
- *U-638* depth-charged by *Loosestrife* on 5/6 May 1943.
- *U-125* rammed by *Oribi* and finished with gun-fire by *snowflake* on 6 May 1943.
- *U-531* depth-charged by *Snowflake* and hit by Hedgehog from *Vidette* on 6 May 1943
- *U-381* depth-charged by *Snowflake* and hit by Hedgehog from *Duncan* on 19 May 1943.
- *U-631* depth-charged by *Sunflower* on 17 October 1943
- *U-274* attacked by aircraft, hit by Hedgehog from *Duncan* on 26 October 1943
- *U-282* Duncan Vidette on 29 october 1943

Table
Source (edited): "http://en.wikipedia.org/wiki/B-7_Escort_Group_(Royal_Navy)"

Battlecruiser Squadron (United Kingdom)

The **Battlecruiser Squadron** was a Royal Navy squadron of battlecruisers that saw service from 1919 to the early part of the Second World War.

Formation

During the First World War, the Royal Navy had initially maintained three squadrons of battlecruisers, until losses at the Battle of Jutland had reduced the number of available battlecruisers sufficiently to warrant a reduction to two squadrons. Following the War, battlecruiser numbers were again reduced to three, with a fourth building.

In late 1919, the Battlecruiser Squadron was formed, consisting of HMS *Tiger*, flagship of Rear Admiral Sir Roger B. Keyes, KCB, KCVO, CMG, along with HMS *Renown* and HMS *Repulse*. HMS *Tiger* was removed from operational service with the commissioning of HMS *Hood* in May 1920, and relegated to a training role. HMS *Hood* then became the flagship of the Battlecruiser Squadron on 18 May 1920.

Special Service Squadron

In 1923, HMS *Hood* and HMS *Repulse*, along with several smaller ships of the First Light Cruiser Squadron, formed part of the Special Service Squadron, under command of Vice-Admiral Sir Frederick Field. The Squadron departed Devonport on 27 November 1923 and returned on 29 September 1924 after travelling around the world.

Inter-War Period

HMS *Hood* was decommissioned for a major overhaul from May 1929 to May 1931. During this period, HMS *Tiger* was returned to active service, to maintain the three ship strength of the squadron. Following her recommissioning, *Hood* again became flagship of the squadron, and remained the flagship until her loss on 24 May 1941. HMS *Tiger* was decommissioned on 30 March 1931 and scrapped shortly after.

Dissolution

HMS *Hood* was lost in combat with the German battleship *Bismarck* at the Battle of Denmark Strait on 24 May 1941. HMS *Repulse* was sunk by Japanese aircraft off Singapore on 10 December 1941. With the loss of the *Hood* and later the *Repulse*, the squadron ceased to exist. HMS *Renown* survived the war and was scrapped in 1948.

Source (edited): "http://en.wikipedia.org/wiki/Battlecruiser_Squadron_(United_Kingdom)"

British Pacific Fleet

The **British Pacific Fleet** (BPF) was a British Commonwealth naval force which saw action against Japan during World War II. The fleet was composed of British Commonwealth naval vessels. The BPF formally came into being on 22 November 1944. Its main base was at Sydney, Australia, with a forward base at Manus Island.

Background

The British Pacific Fleet was, and remains, the most powerful conventional war fleet assembled by the Royal Navy. By VJ Day it included four battleships, eighteen aircraft carriers, eleven cruisers and many smaller warships and support vessels. Despite this, it was dwarfed by the forces that the United States had in action against Japan. While the British fleet was not critical to the war in the Pacific, it did participate in and protect the flank of the final Allied drive against Japan in 1945.

Following their retreat to the western side of the Indian Ocean in 1942, British naval forces did not return to the South West Pacific theatre until 17 May 1944, when an Anglo-American carrier task force implemented Operation Transom, a joint raid on Surabaya, Java.

The U.S. was liberating British territories in the Pacific and extending its influence. It was therefore seen as a political and military imperative to restore a British presence in the region and to deploy British military assets directly against Japan. The British government were determined that British territories, such as Hong Kong, should be recaptured by British forces.

The British establishment, however, was not unanimous on the commitment of the BPF. Churchill, in particular, argued against it, not wishing to be a visibly junior partner in what had been exclusively the United States' battle. (The Australian and New Zealand forces that were active had been absorbed into US command structures.) He also considered that a British presence would be unwelcome and should be concentrated on Burma and Malaya. Naval planners, supported by the Chiefs of Staff, believed that such a commitment would strengthen British influence and the British Chiefs of Staff considered mass resignation, so strongly held were their opinions. Some U.S. planners had also considered, in 1944, that a strong British presence against Japan was essential to an early end to the war and American home opinion would also be badly affected if Britain did not put itself in the line.

The Admiralty had proposed an active British role in the Pacific in early 1944 but the initial USN response had been discouraging. Admiral Ernest King, Commander-in-Chief United States Fleet and Chief of Naval Operations, and alleged Anglophobe, was reluctant to concede any such role and raised a number of issues, including the requirement that the BPF should be entirely self-sufficient. These were eventually overcome or discounted and, when at a meeting, U.S. President Franklin D. Roosevelt "intervened to say that the British Fleet was no sooner offered than accepted. In this, though the fact was not mentioned, he overruled Admiral King's opinion".

The Australian Government had sought U.S. military assistance in 1942, when it was faced with the possibility of Japanese invasion. While Australia had made a significant contribution to the Pacific War, it had never been an equal partner with its U.S. counterparts in strategic decision-making. It was argued that a British presence would act as a counter-balance to the powerful and increasing U.S. presence in the Pacific.

Constituent forces

The fleet was founded when Admiral Sir Bruce Fraser struck his flag at Trincomalee as Commander-in-Chief of the British Eastern Fleet and hoisted it in the gunboat HMS *Tarantula* as Commander-in-Chief British Pacific Fleet. He later transferred his flag to a more suitable vessel, the battleship HMS *Howe*.

The Eastern Fleet was reorganised into the British East Indies Fleet, based in Ceylon (now Sri Lanka), and what was to be become the British Pacific Fleet (BPF). The BPF operated against targets in Sumatra, gaining experience until early 1945, when it departed Trincomalee for Sydney. (These operations are described in the article on the British Eastern Fleet.)

The name "British Pacific Fleet" is misleading, the BPF was multi-national although the British provided the majority of the fleet and all the capital ships. It eventually comprised ships and personnel from the British Royal Navy (RN), British Royal Fleet Auxiliary (RFA), Royal Australian Navy (RAN), Royal Canadian Navy (RCN) and Royal New Zealand Navy (RNZN). The RAN's contribution was limited because its larger vessels had been integrated with United States Navy formations since 1942. A high proportion of naval aviators were New Zealanders. The USN also contributed to the BPF, as did personnel from the South African Navy (SAN). Australian and New Zealand ports and infrastructure also made vital contributions in support of the BPF.

During World War II, the fleet was commanded by Admiral Sir Bruce Fraser. In practice, command of the fleet in action devolved to Vice-Admiral Sir Bernard Rawlings, with Vice-Admiral Sir Philip Vian in charge of air operations by the Royal Navy's Fleet Air Arm (FAA). The fighting end of the fleet was referred to as Task Force 37 or 57 and the Fleet Train was Task Force 113.

Fleet Logistics

Melbourne, 13 December 1944. First conference of the staff of Admiral Sir Bruce Fraser's new British Pacific Fleet, held in Melbourne. Left to right: Lieutenant Commander G. P. Vollmer (Secretary to Chief of Staff); Lieutenant Commander R. N. Heard; Vice-Admiral C. S. Daniel (seated) Vice Admiral (Administration); Commodore W. G. Andrews; Captain E. H. Shattock (concealed); Captain R. C. Duckworth; Lieutenant S. G. Warrender.

The deployment of the BPF would not be straightforward. The Pacific war environment with its enormous distances and fast paced carrier operations was unfamiliar to the Royal Navy. It was a radically different operating environment requiring warships to remain at sea for extended periods, without ready access to land bases. Britain had previously depended on land bases for replenishment, and had to develop a fleet train to support its efforts at sea, far away from British bases. The technical implications may well have been better appreciated by Admiral King - a naval aviator - than by his British colleagues.

The requirement that the BPF be self-sufficient necessitated the establishment of a fleet train that could adequately support an active naval force at sea for weeks or months. The Royal Navy had been used to operating close to its bases in Britain, the Mediterranean or the Indian Ocean, and purpose-built infrastructure and expertise were lacking. Indeed, in the north Atlantic and Mediterranean, the high risks of submarine and air attack would have made routine at-sea refuelling highly dangerous. Fortunately for the BPF "the American logistics authorities... interpreted self-sufficiency in a very liberal sense".

The Admiralty sent Vice Admiral C. S. Daniel to the United States for consultation about the supply and administration of the fleet. He then proceeded to Australia where he became Vice Admiral, Administration, British Pacific Fleet, a role that "if unspectacular compared with command of a fighting squadron, was certainly one of the most arduous to be allocated to a British Flag officer during the entire war." The US Pacific Fleet had assembled an enormous fleet of oilers and supply ships of every type. Even before the war, it had been active in the development of underway replenishment techniques. The Admiralty realised that it had a great deal of new capabilities to develop, in a short time, and with whatever it had to hand. Lacking purpose-built ships, it had to assemble a fleet train from whatever RN, RFA or merchant ships were available. On 8 February 1944 the First Sea Lord, Admiral of the Fleet Sir Alan Cunningham, informed the Defence Committee that 91 ships would be required to support the BPF. This was based on an assumption that the BPF would be active off the Philippines, or would have a base there. By March, the war zone had moved north and the Americans were unwilling to allow the British to establish facilities in the Philippines. The estimate had grown to 158 ships, as it was recognised that operations eventually would be fought close to Japan. This had to be balanced against the shipping needed to import food for the civilian population of the UK. In January 1945, the War cabinet was forced to postpone the deployment of the fleet by two months due to the shortage of shipping.

The BPF found that its tankers were too few in number, too slow, and in some cases unsuitable for the task of replenishment at sea. Its oiling gear, hoses, and fittings were too often poorly designed. British ships refuelled at sea mostly by the over-the-stern method, a safer but less efficient technique compared with the American method of re-fuelling alongside. Lack of proper equipment and insufficient practice meant burst hoses or excessive time at risk to submarine attack while holding a constant course during fuelling. Moreover, as the Royal Australian Navy had already discovered, British built ships had only about a third of the refrigeration space of a comparable American ship. British ships therefore required replenishment more frequently than American ships. In some cases even American-built equipment was not interchangeable, for FAA aircraft had been "Anglicized" by the installation of British radios and oxygen masks, while British Corsairs had their wing-folding arrangements modified in order to fit into the more cramped hangars of British carriers. Replacement aircraft therefore had to be brought from the UK.

The British Chiefs of Staff decided early on to base the BPF in Australia rather than India, where there was famine and unrest over British colonial rule. While it was apparent that Australia, with its population of only about seven million could not support the projected 675,000 men and women of the BPF, the actual extent of the Australian contribution was undetermined. The Australian government agreed to contribute to the support of the BPF, but the Australian economy was fully committed to the war effort, and manpower and stores for the BPF could only come from taking them from American and Australian forces fighting the Japanese. Unfortunately, Admiral Sir Bruce Fraser arrived in Sydney on 10 December 1944 under the mistaken impression that Australia had asked for the BPF and promised to provide for its needs. Two days later, the Acting Prime Minister of Australia Frank Forde announced the allocation of £21,156,500 for the maintenance of the BPF. In January 1945, General of the Army Douglas MacArthur agreed to release American stockpiles in Australia to support the BPF. The Australian government soon became concerned at the voracious demands of the BPF works program, which was criticised by Australian military leaders. In April 1945, Fraser publicly criticised the Australian government's handling of waterside industrial disputes that were holding up British ships. The government was shocked and angered, but agreed to allocate £6,562,500 for BPF naval works. Fraser was not satisfied. On 8 August 1945 Prime Minister of the United Kingdom Clement Attlee felt obliged to express his regret for the misunderstandings to the Australian government.

The distance from Sydney was too far to allow efficient fleet support, so, with much American support, a forward base was established at Manus atoll, in the Admiralty Islands, which was described as "Scapa Flow with bloody palm trees."

As well as its base at Sydney, the Fleet Air Arm established Mobile Naval Air Bases (MONABs) in Australia to provide technical and logistic support for the aircraft. The first of these became active in Sydney in January 1945.

Active service

Royal Navy Fleet Air Arm Avengers, Seafires and Fireflies on the deck of HMS *Implacable* warm up their engines before taking off. Other British warships can be seen in the background.

Major actions in which the fleet was involved included Operation Meridian, air strikes in January 1945 against oil production at Palembang, Sumatra. These raids, conducted in bad weather, succeeded in reducing the oil supply of the Japanese Navy. A total of 48 FAA aircraft was lost due to enemy action and crash landings; they claimed 30 Japanese planes destroyed in dogfights and 38 on the ground.

The United States Navy (USN), which had control of Allied operations in the Pacific Ocean Areas, gave the BPF combat units the designation of Task Force 57 (TF-57) when it joined Admiral Raymond Spruance's United States Fifth Fleet on 15 March 1945. On 27 May 1945, it became Task Force 37 (TF-37) when it became part of Admiral William Halsey's United States Third Fleet.

In March 1945, while supporting the invasion of Okinawa, the BPF had sole responsibility for operations in the Sakishima Islands. Its role was to suppress Japanese air activity, using gunfire and air attack, at potential Kamikaze staging airfields that would otherwise be a threat to U.S. Navy vessels operating at Okinawa. The carriers were subject to heavy and repeated kamikaze attacks, but because of their armoured flight decks, the British aircraft carriers proved highly resistant (unlike their U.S. counterparts), and returned to action relatively quickly. The U.S.N liaison officer on the *Indefatigable* commented: "*When a kamikaze hits a U.S. carrier it means 6 months of repair at Pearl [Harbor]. When a kamikaze hits a Limey carrier it's just a case of "Sweepers, man your brooms."*" (Subsequent studies, however, showed that serious damage had occurred to the ships' structure and post-war modernisation was uneconomic. .)

HMS *Victorious* on fire after a Kamikaze hit.

Fleet Air Arm Supermarine Seafires saw service in the Pacific campaigns. Due to their good high altitude performance and lack of ordnance-carrying capabilities (compared to the Hellcats and Corsairs of the Fleet) the Seafires were allocated the vital defensive duties of Combat Air Patrol (CAP) over the fleet. Seafires were thus heavily involved in countering the Kamikaze attacks during the Iwo Jima landings and beyond. The Seafires' best day was 15 August 1945, shooting down eight attacking aircraft for a single loss.

In April 1945, the British 4th Submarine Flotilla was transferred to the major Allied submarine base at Fremantle, Western Australia, as part of BPF. Its most notable success in this period was the sinking of the heavy cruiser *Ashigara*, on 8 June 1945 in Banka Strait, off Sumatra, by HMS *Trenchant* and HMS *Stygian*. On 31 July 1945, in Operation Struggle, the British midget submarine *XE3*, crewed by Lieutenant Ian Fraser, Acting Leading Seaman James Magennis, Sub-Lieutenant William James Lanyon Smith, RNZNVR, and Engine Room Artificer Third Class, Charles Alfred Reed, attacked Japanese shipping at Singapore. They sank the heavy cruiser *Takao*, which settled to the bottom at its berth. Fraser and Magennis were both awarded the Victoria Cross, Smith received the Distinguished Service Order (DSO) and Reed the Conspicuous Gallantry Medal (CGM).

Battleships and aircraft from the fleet also attacked the Japanese home islands. The battleship *King George V* bombarded naval installations at Hamamatsu, near Tokyo; the last time a British battleship fired in action. Meanwhile, carrier strikes were carried out against land and harbour targets including, notably, the disabling of a Japanese escort carrier by British naval aircraft. Although, during the assaults on Japan, the British commanders had accepted that the BPF should become a component element of the U.S. 3rd Fleet, the U.S. fleet commander, William Halsey, excluded British forces from a raid on Kure naval base on political grounds. Halsey later wrote, in his memoirs: "*it was imperative that we forestall a possible postwar claim by Britain that she had delivered even a part of the final blow that demolished the Japanese fleet.... an exclusively American attack was therefore in American interests.*"

The BPF would have played a major

part in a proposed invasion of the Japanese home islands, known as Operation Downfall, which was cancelled after Japan surrendered. The last naval air action in World War II was on VJ-Day when British carrier aircraft shot down Japanese Zero fighters.

Lt Robert Hampton Gray, a Canadian naval airman who piloted a Vought Corsair with 1841 Naval Air Squadron on HMS *Formidable*, was awarded the Victoria Cross, following his death in an attack on a Japanese destroyer at Onagawa Wan, Japan, on August 9, 1945.

Fighter squadrons from the fleet claimed a total of 112.5 Japanese aircraft shot down. 1844 Squadron NAS (flying Hellcats) was the top-scoring squadron, with 28 claims.

Allied co-operation

The conflicting British and American political objectives have been mentioned: Britain needed to "show the flag" in an effective way while the U.S. wished to demonstrate, beyond question, its own pre-eminence in the Pacific. In practice, there were cordial relations between the fighting fleets and their sea commanders. Although Admiral King had stipulated that the BPF should be wholly self-sufficient, in practice, material assistance was freely given: American officers told Rear Admiral Douglas Fisher, commander of the British Fleet Train, that he could have anything and everything *"that could be given without Admiral King's knowledge."*

Post-war

Following the end of hostilities, the fleet formed the naval arm of the British Commonwealth Occupation Force in Japan.

The effort made by Britain and its Commonwealth partners in the final stages of the Pacific war did manage to repair British prestige and influence in this region which it had been forced to neglect while concentrating on the war in Europe.

Order of battle

The fleet included 17 aircraft carriers (with 300 aircraft), four battleships, 10 cruisers, 40 destroyers, 18 sloops, 13 frigates, 35 minesweepers, other kinds of fighting ships, and many support vessels.

Fleet Air Arm Squadrons
(Sources:)
(See List of Fleet Air Arm carrier air groups)
Source (edited): "http://en.wikipedia.org/wiki/British_Pacific_Fleet"

Eastern Fleet

The British **Eastern Fleet** (also known as the **East Indies Fleet** and the **Far East Fleet**) was a fleet of the Royal Navy which existed from 1941 to 1971. In 1904 First Sea Lord Sir John Fisher ordered that in the event of war the three main commands in the Far East, the East Indies Squadron, the China Squadron and the Australian Squadron, should all come under one command called the Eastern Fleet based in Singapore. The Commander-in-Chief on the China Station would then take command. During World War I the squadrons remained distinct commands and Eastern Fleet was used only as a general term. The three squadron structure continued until World War II and the beginning of hostilities with the Empire of Japan, when the Eastern Fleet was formally constituted on 8 December 1941, amalgamating the East Indies Squadron and the China Squadron. During the war, it included many ships and personnel from other navies, including the Royal Netherlands Navy, Royal Australian Navy, the Royal New Zealand Navy and the United States Navy. With the creation of the British Pacific Fleet in 1944/1945, the Eastern Fleet became the East Indies Fleet until the end of the war, when it became the Far East Fleet and operated in all Far East areas including parts of the Pacific Ocean.

Background

Until World War II, the Indian Ocean had been a British "lake". It was ringed by significant British and Commonwealth possessions and much of the strategic supplies needed in peace and war had to pass across it: Persian oil, Malayan rubber, Indian tea, Australian and New Zealand foodstuffs. Britain also utilized Australian and New Zealand manpower; hence, safe passage for British cargo ships was critical.

Despite this, the Royal Navy had tended to station its older ships in the east and use the China Station and the Far East Station as a source of reinforcements for other theatres. Even when gravely threatened, the Eastern Fleet largely consisted of older capital ships too slow and vulnerable to be of use in the Atlantic or Mediterranean.

At the outbreak of World War II, the German Navy (*Kriegsmarine*) used auxiliary cruisers (converted merchant ships) and the Pocket Battleship *Graf Spee* to threaten the sea lanes and tie down the Royal Navy. In mid-1940, Italy declared war and the Italian vessels based in Italian East Africa posed a threat to the supply routes through the Red Sea. Worse was to come when the Japanese declared war in December 1941 and, after Pearl Harbor, the sinking of *Prince of Wales* and *Repulse*, and the occupation of Malaya, Singapore, and the Dutch East Indies, there was an aggressive threat from the east.

This became reality when an overwhelming Japanese naval force operated in the eastern Indian Ocean, sinking an aircraft carrier, other warships and disrupting freight traffic along the Indian east coast. At this stage, the Chief of the Imperial General Staff, General Sir Alan Brooke wrote:

We were hanging by our eyelids! Australia and India were threatened by the Japanese, we had temporarily lost control of the Indian Ocean, the Germans were threatening Iran and our oil, Auchinleck was in precarious straits in the desert, and the submarine sinkings were heavy.

The fear was that a concerted Japanese stroke could chase the Royal Navy from the Indian Ocean, with dire implications for India, and that German success in the Caucasus and in Egypt would threaten the Persian Gulf.

Early war years

Until 1941, the main threat to British interests in the region was the presence of German commerce raiders (auxiliary cruisers) and submarines. The fleet had trade protection as its first priority and was required to escort convoys and eliminate the raiders. The Germans had converted merchant ships to act as commerce raiders and allocated supply ships to maintain them. The location and destruction of these German raiders consumed much British naval effort until the last raider - *Michel* - was sunk in October 1943.

On 10 June 1940, the entry of Italy into the war introduced a new threat to the oil supply routes from the Persian Gulf, which passed through the Red Sea to the Mediterranean. The Italians controlled ports in Italian East Africa and Tiensin, China. The Italian Royal Navy (*Regia Marina*) presence in the Red Sea, Indian Ocean, and the western Pacific Ocean consisted of destroyers, submarines, and a small number of armed merchantmen. The majority of these were based at Massawa in Eritrea as part of the Italian Red Sea Flotilla, primarily seven destroyers and eight submarines. During the course of 1940, the Red Sea Flotilla lost four submarines and one destroyer during early attempts to intercept British convoys in the Red Sea.

The Italian naval forces in East Africa were caught in a vice. To put to sea invited heavy British reaction, while to stay in ports threatened by British and Commonwealth forces became impossible. In 1941, during the East African Campaign, these ports were captured by the British. The Italians attempted to break out to German-occupied Europe, to the Vichy French colony of Madagascar, to Japan, to Tianjin, China, or to any other neutral port where they might find refuge.

Some of these breakout attempts were successful. Four Italian submarines successfully reached Bordeaux, two out of three of the Italian armed merchantmen reached Kobe, Japan, and a few other vessels made it to other Axis-friendly ports. The rest of the Italian vessels in East Africa were captured, sunk, or scuttled. Six Italian destroyers attempted to attack Port Suez and Port Sudan, but all six were lost due to a combination of British air and sea forces and scuttling by their own crews. In actions against the Italians, the Eastern Fleet lost two destroyers and a sloop.

The Eastern Fleet also supported British and Commonwealth ground forces in their actions in Iraq (Operation *Sabine*) and Iran (Operation Countenance).

Singapore

Before the fall of Singapore, the Eastern Fleet's naval base at Singapore (HMNB Singapore) was part of the British Far East Command.

British Far East defence planning was based on two assumptions. The first assumption was that the United States would remain as an effective ally in the western Pacific Ocean, with a fleet based at Singapore, and that the Philippines would be available as a forward base for British warships. Secondly, it was assumed that the technical capabilities and aggression of the Imperial Japanese Navy were over-estimated. In these circumstances, with the Japanese fleet engaged by the United States Navy (USN), the Admiralty sent the four obsolescent *Revenge* class battleships to Singapore to provide defensive firepower and a British presence. The British assumptions were destroyed on 7 December 1941: the impact of the Japanese attack on Pearl Harbor denied substantial USN support to the British defence of the "Malay barrier" and made impossible the relief of American garrisons in the Philippines. Furthermore, Japanese capabilities exceeded expectations.

After the fall of France in June 1940, Japanese pressure on the Vichy authorities in French Indochina resulted in the granting of base and transit rights, albeit with significant restrictions. Despite this, in September 1940, the Japanese launched an invasion of French Indochina. The bases thus acquired in Indochina allowed extended Japanese air coverage of the invasion forces bound for Malaya and for the Dutch East Indies. In these circumstances, the *Prince of Wales* and *Repulse* were vulnerable to concerted air attacks from the Japanese bases in Indochina and, without air cover, they were sunk in December 1941. The modern aircraft carrier HMS *Indomitable* had been intended to be part of the squadron, but accidental damage prevented this. It's unlikely that the limited naval air cover thus available would have protected the squadron and the *Indomitable* might also have been a loss.

After the sinking of *Prince of Wales* and *Repulse* and the death of Admiral Sir Tom Phillips, Admiral Sir Geoffrey Layton assumed command of the Eastern Fleet. The fleet withdrew first to Java and, following the Fall of Singapore, to Trincomalee, Ceylon (now Sri Lanka). In March 1942, Admiral Sir James Somerville arrived in Ceylon and assumed command from Layton.

Indian Ocean retreat

When Admiral Somerville inspected the base at Trincomalee, its deficiencies were clear to him. He found the port inadequate, vulnerable to a determined attack, and open to spying. An isolated island base with a safe, deep anchorage in a suitably strategic position was required. Addu Atoll met the requirements and it was secretly developed as a fleet anchorage. Once available, the facilities at Addu Atoll were used extensively by the Royal Navy.

The Eastern Fleet was divided into two: Force A and Force B. Force A consisted of the modernised HMS *Warspite* and the two available fleet aircraft carriers. Force B was based on the slow *Revenge* class battleships of the 3rd Battle Squadron, based at the fleet's new operational base at Kilindini near Mombasa in Kenya and relatively safe from the Japanese fleet. Neither individually nor together could the two Eastern Fleet forces challenge a determined Japanese naval assault.

Following the Japanese capture of the Andaman Islands, the main elements of the Fleet retreated to Addu Atoll in Maldives. Then, following Chuichi Nagumo's Indian Ocean raid and raid on Ceylon in early 1942, the Fleet moved its operational base to Kilindini near Mombasa in Kenya, as their more forward fleet anchorages could not be adequately protected from Japanese attack. The fleet in the Indian Ocean was then gradually reduced to little more than a convoy escort force as other commitments called for the more modern powerful ships.

In May 1942, the Eastern Fleet supported the invasion of Madagascar, **Operation Ironclad**. This was an operation aimed at thwarting any attempt by Japanese vessels to use naval bases on the Vichy French controlled territory. During the invasion, vessels of the Eastern Fleet were confronted by vessels of the French Navy (two armed merchant cruisers, two sloops, and five submarines) and submarines of the Imperial Japanese Navy (I-10, I-16, I-18, and I-20 and midget submarines M-16b and M-20b).

Indian Ocean strikes

After the departure of the main battle forces during February 1944, the Indian Ocean was left with mostly escort carriers and older battleships as the core of its naval forces. Allied advances in the Mediterranean and northern Europe during 1943 and 1944, however, released naval resources. As a result, more British aircraft carriers entered the area; plus the battlecruiser HMS *Renown*, battleships *Howe*, *Queen Elizabeth*, *Valiant* and supporting warships.

Preparations were put in hand for a more aggressive stance in the Indian Ocean and for British naval participation in the Pacific theatre. Agreement had been reached, after objections from Admiral Ernest King, but new procedures would need to be learnt by naval crews and Fleet Air Arm (FAA) aircrew. To this end, Operation Diplomat, a training exercise, took place in late March, 1944. The objective was for the fleet to rendezvous with a group of tankers (escorted by HNLMS *Tromp*) and practice refuelling at sea procedures. They then rendezvoused with United States Navy Task Force 58.5, the USS *Saratoga* and three destroyers, and returned to Trincomalee on 31 March. The U.S. task force had been detached to the Indian Ocean to bolster local air defences and also to impart necessary procedures to FAA aircrew, which was done over two or three days' intensive activity at sea. Sources for the dates of return to Trincomalee and the joint US/UK training differ.

Admiral King then requested that, during April, the Eastern Fleet should engage Japanese forces in their area and hold them there to reduce the opposition to an American seaborne assault on Hollandia (now Jayapura) and Aitape on the north coast of Netherlands New Guinea. An airborne attack by the Eastern Fleet (including Task Force 58.5) on Sabang, off Sumatra was executed (Operation Cockpit). Surprise was achieved: military and oil installations were heavily damaged by the attacks, aggravating Japanese fuel shortages. The American involvement was extended to capitalise on the success with a second attack, this time on Surabaya, eastern Java, on 17 May (Operation Transom). The distances for this operation necessitated replenishment at sea. Again, the defenders were unprepared and significant damage was made to port, military and oil infrastructure. After this, on 18 May, *Saratoga* and her destroyers returned to the Pacific after what Admiral Somerville called "*a profitable and very happy association of Task Group 58.5 with the Eastern Fleet*".

At the end of August 1944, Admiral Somerville was relieved as Commander-in-Chief Eastern Fleet by Admiral Sir Bruce Fraser, former Commander-in-Chief Home Fleet. Somerville had been Commander-in-Chief Eastern Fleet since March 1942. During this time, there had been friction between him and the Supreme Allied Commander South East Asia Theatre, Louis Mountbatten. The need for an influential military representative in Washington provided the opportunity for a change. Fraser later transferred his flag to the newly-formed British Pacific Fleet on 22 November 1944.

By this time, the Eastern Fleet included ships from Britain, Australia, New Zealand, the Netherlands and France, and became the East Indies Fleet.

The Eastern Fleet was greatly augmented by units intended for the Pacific and, on 4 January 1945 two British carriers (HMS *Indomitable* and *Indefatigable*) made an attack on oil refineries at Pangkalan Brandon in Sumatra (Operation Lentil).

The final attacks were flown as Force 63 was en route for Sydney, Australia to become the British Pacific Fleet. Operation *Meridian One* and Operation *Meridian Two* were air attacks upon the oil refineries at Pladjoe, north of Palembang, Java and at Soengei Gerong, Sumatra. Although successful these were not as smooth as earlier attacks. Poor weather delayed fly-offs for both raids, 48 aircraft were lost or damaged and refuelling at sea was only completed with difficulty and damage due to poor weather and lack of expertise.

A number of Fleet Air Arm pilots were captured by the Japanese during the Palembang raid. These were taken to Singapore where at least some of them were executed by the Japanese military authorities.

Important operations were launched in 1945 as the East Indies Fleet in the recapture of Burma, including landings on Ramree Island and Akyab and near Rangoon and diversionary operations (Operation Bishop).

On May 15–16, 1945, the British executed Operation Dukedom and the 26th Destroyer Flotilla (HMS *Saumarez*, *Venus*, *Verulam*, *Vigilant* and *Virago*) sank the Japanese heavy cruiser *Haguro* in the Malacca Straits by torpedo attack.

Trade protection

This was the protection of merchant ships in the Indian Ocean and it was seen as the Eastern Fleet's primary role. The threats were German, Italian and Japanese submarines, German warships and Italian and German auxiliary cruisers. A substantial part of the Fleet was employed in escorting convoys and hunting submarines and surface ships and their supply vessels. For much of the war, with naval resources needed elsewhere, there were barely enough warships to perform these tasks and, without escorts, the battleships and aircraft carriers that remained could not safely be used.

Postwar

After the war, the Fleet was once again based at Singapore Naval Base and took part in the Malayan Emergency and the Confrontation with Indonesia in the 1960s. By 1964 the fleet on station included HMS *Victorious*, HMS *Centaur*, HMS *Bulwark*, HMS *Kent*, HMS *Hampshire*, seventeen destroyers and frigates, some drawn from the Mediterranean, about ten minesweepers and five submarines. *Kent* and *Victorious* helped to fill gaps in Singapore's radar cover by providing additional early warning.

The Flag Officer Second-in-Command Far East Fleet, for most of the postwar period a Rear Admiral, was based afloat, and tasked with keeping the fleet 'up to the mark operationally,' while the fleet commander, a Vice Admiral, ran the fleet programme and major items of administration 'including all provision for docking and maintenance' from his base in Singapore. Jack Scatchard (1962–64) and Terence Lewin, as Rear Admirals, were among those who held this appointment.

The Fleet was disbanded in 1971, and on October 31, 1971, the last day of the validity of the Anglo-Malayan Defence Agreement, the last Commander, Far East Fleet, Rear Admiral Anthony Troup, hauled down his flag. That day, he took the salute aboard from RFA *Stromness* from his final remaining ships. Led by HMS *Glamorgan*, flying the flag of Flag Officer Second-in-Command Far East Fleet, the frigates HMS *Scylla*, HMS *Argonaut*, HMS *Gurkha*, HMS *Arethusa*, and HMS *Danae*, sailed past, along with the repair ship HMS *Triumph* and six Royal Fleet Auxiliaries. The Fleet was replaced by a small ANZUK naval squadron comprising British, Australian, and New Zealand ships.

List of ships

During World War II, the British Eastern Fleet included, from time to time, a number of warships from other Allied nations, such as Australia (Royal Australian Navy), France (Free French Navy), the Netherlands (Royal Netherlands Navy), India (Royal Indian Navy), New Zealand (Royal New Zealand Navy), and the United States. Major ships attached to the Eastern Fleet, or where indicated, East Indies Fleet, included:

- HMS *Hermes* - Sunk 9 April 1942
- HMS *Illustrious* - Aircraft Carrier in Eastern Fleet 1944, arriving January 1944
- HMS *Victorious* - Aircraft Carrier in Eastern Fleet, arriving July 1944
- HMS *Indomitable* - Aircraft Carrier in Eastern Fleet 1944, arriving July 1944
- HMS *Renown* - Battlecruiser in Eastern Fleet 1944
- HMS *Queen Elizabeth* - Battleship in Eastern Fleet 1944, East Indies Fleet 1945
- HMS *Valiant* - Battleship in Eastern Fleet 1944
- French Battleship *Richelieu* - Battleship in Eastern Fleet 1944, East Indies Fleet 1945
- HMS *Howe* - Battleship in Eastern Fleet August 1944 - November 1944
- Submarines: 2nd Flotilla, of approx eight "S" class and four "T" class
- HMS *Prince of Wales* - Sunk 10 December 1941
- HMS *Repulse* - Sunk 10 December 1941
- HMS *Electra* - Sunk 27 February 1942
- HMS *Express*
- HMS *Cornwall* - Sunk 5 April 1942
- HMS *Dorsetshire* - Sunk 5 April 1942
- HMAS *Vampire* - Sunk 9 April 1942
- HMS *Adamant* - Submarine Depot Ship
- USS *Saratoga*

Commanders-in-Chief

Commanders-in-Chief have included:
Commander-in-Chief, Eastern Fleet
- 1941 - 1942 Vice-Admiral Sir Geoffrey Layton
- 1942 - 1944 Vice-Admiral Sir James Somerville
- 1944 Vice-Admiral Sir Bruce Fraser

Commander-in-Chief, East Indies Fleet
- 1944 - 1945 Vice-Admiral Sir Arthur Power
- 1945 - 1946 Vice-Admiral Sir Clement Moody
- 1946 - 1948 Vice-Admiral Sir Arthur Palliser
- 1948 - 1950 Vice-Admiral Sir Charles Woodhouse
- 1950 - 1952 Vice-Admiral Sir Geoffrey Oliver

Commander-in-Chief, Far East Fleet
- 1952 - 1953 Vice-Admiral Sir Guy Russell
- 1953 - 1954 Vice-Admiral Sir Charles Lambe
- 1954 - 1955 Vice-Admiral Sir Charles Norris
- 1955 - 1957 Vice-Admiral Sir Alan Scott-Moncrieff
- 1957 - 1960 Vice-Admiral Sir Gerald Gladstone
- 1960 - 1962 Vice-Admiral Sir David Luce
- 1962 - 1965 Vice-Admiral Sir Desmond Dreyer
- 1965 - 1967 Vice-Admiral Sir Frank Twiss
- 1967 - 1969 Vice-Admiral Sir William O'Brien
- 1969 - 1971 Vice-Admiral Sir Derek Empson
- 1971 Rear-Admiral Sir Anthony Troup

Source (edited): "http://en.wikipedia.org/wiki/Eastern_Fleet"

Escort Group (naval)

Escort Groups for convoy protection were a British development in the war at sea during World War II. They were a tactical innovation by the Royal Navy in anti-submarine warfare, to combat the threat of the German Navy's "wolfpack" tactics. Escort Groups consisted of mixed types of small warships that operated together as a permanent team, defending shipping convoys during World War II, and more particularly, during the Battle of the Atlantic. The development of these 'escort groups' proved an effective means of defending shipping convoys. They were rigorously trained in anti-submarine tactics and had many successes. For example, in a ten-day period in 1941, four U-boats were sunk with the loss of three of Germany's top U-boat commanders.

Background

During the first year of the Battle of the Atlantic British convoy protection was the responsibility of the Western Approaches Command, based first in Plymouth, then, as the focus of the campaign moved after the Fall of France, in Liverpool..

Western Approaches Command controlled an array of escort vessels, mainly elderly destroyers, sloops, trawlers and, later, corvettes to escort merchant ships travelling to and from Britain. These were not numerous enough or sufficiently long ranged to provide a full escort service across the Atlantic, but would accompany convoys to and from meeting points at the edge of the Western Approaches, at points thought to be beyond U-boat range.

In the beginning convoy escorts were compiled on an ad hoc basis; the escorts would be dispatched as and when available, and arrive singly or in small groups. Command of the escort force fell to the senior officer present, and could change as each new ship arrived. Any tactical arrangements had to be made on the spot, and communicated by signal lamp to each ship in turn. The ships would be un-co-ordinated, being unused to working together, and would have no common battle plan or tactics.

These deficiencies led to a major defeat in October 1940 when Convoy HX 79 was savaged by a wolfpack of 5 U-boats. Despite an escort of 11 warships, 12 ships were sunk from the convoy, while the U-boats were unscathed.

This disaster gaver the impetus for Percy Noble, the commander of WAC, to form discrete groups; by the beginning of 1941 eight groups had been formed.

Service history

In 1941 WAC had 8 escort groups formed. These typically comprised 6 to 8 ships, under the command of an RN officer, usually a Commander or Lt Cdr. By operating together under a single commander, groups were able to develop group tactics and practice their use; with the issue of a single short command the various ships of the group, often out of sight of each other, could be relied upon to act in a co-ordinated fashion. Later these tactics were standardized and taught to all escort group commanders at the Western Approaches Tactical Unit.

This level of teamwork was never achieved by the attacking U-Boats. Although the wolfpack was a co-ordinated in that a number of boats would be concentrated on a target convoy, once gathered the boats would attack individually without any attempt at further co-operation. It was not unknown for U-boats to get in each others way whilst attacking, or collide with each other. Time and again during the Battle of the Atlantic relatively small, well-handled escort groups were able to frustrate attacks by more numerous groups of U-boats, and ensure the "safe and timely arrival" of their charges. In one example, in November 1942, Convoy ON 144 of 33 ships protected by the B-6 Escort Group of just 5 corvettes, were attacked by a group of 10 U-boats. Over the next three days they fought off attacks by the wolfpack for the loss of 5 ships and one corvette. 28 ships arrived safely. Following this action the SOE (Senior Officer Escort) was "warmly congratulated" for preventing what could have been a major disaster, and the contrast with HX 79 was apparent.
Source (edited): "http://en.wikipedia.org/wiki/Escort_Group_(naval)"

Force H

Force H was a British naval formation during the Second World War. It was formed in 1940 to replace French naval power in the western Mediterranean that had been removed by the French armistice with Nazi Germany.

It occupied an odd place within the naval chain of command. Normal British practice was to have various naval stations and fleets around the world whose commanders reported to the First Sea Lord. Force H was based at Gibraltar, and there was already a flag officer at the base, Flag Officer Commanding, North Atlantic. However, the commanding officer of Force H did not report to this officer; he reported directly to the First Sea Lord.

Operation Catapult

One of the first operations that Force H took part in was connected with the reason for its formation. French naval power still existed in the Mediterranean, and the British Government viewed it as a threat to British interests. It was feared that the Vichy government of Pétain would hand the ships over to Germany, despite a vow that that would never happen. Such an incidence would almost certainly decisively tip the balance against Britain in the Mediterranean. Consequently, Force H was ordered to execute Operation Catapult.

The most powerful of the remaining French forces was in port at Mers-el-Kébir in Algeria. It consisted of the French fast battleships *Strasbourg* and *Dunkerque*, two of the most modern and powerful units in the French fleet and two older battleships, along with escorting vessels. Force H steamed to off the Algerian coast, and an envoy was sent to the French commander. Various terms were offered, including internment of the fleet in a neutral country, joining the British forces and scuttling the fleet at its berths. However, the commander of the French forces reported only the scuttling option to his superiors. He was thus ordered to fight. The reasons for the omission have been debated by many. It is often thought that the anti-British bias of the French commander was to blame.

The result of action was that the remains of the French fleet escaped to Toulon, a French base on the Mediterranean coast of metropolitan France. They did so at heavy cost. The old French battleship *Bretagne* blew up under British gunfire, killing over 1,000 French sailors. The old battleship *Provence* was also heavily damaged and *Strasbourg* and *Dunkerque* were also hit, though *Strasbourg* escaped with four destroyers.

Convoy operations

After this unpleasant operation, Force H settled down to its more normal operations. These involved general naval tasks in the western basin of the Mediterranean. Prominent amongst these tasks was fighting convoys through to Malta. The early convoys came through with relatively light losses. That changed in 1941, when the Germans sent the *Luftwaffe*'s X. *Fliegerkorps* to Sicily. Its bombers took a dreadful toll of both warships and merchantmen.

In November 1940, screening convoys to Malta, Force H made an important contribution to Operation MB8, and the resulting success of Operation Judgement.

"Sink the *Bismarck*!"

The most famous incident involving Force H in 1941 did not occur in the Mediterranean, but in the Atlantic Ocean. The battleship *Bismarck* had sailed in company with the heavy cruiser *Prinz Eugen* from Germany to commerce raid in the Atlantic. She went round far to the north of the UK, passing through the Denmark Strait between Iceland and Greenland. There, she was intercepted by a powerful British force made up of the new battleship *Prince of Wales* and the old battlecruiser *Hood*. The engagement was a disaster for the Royal Navy, with *Prince of Wales* being damaged and *Hood* blowing up. Only three out of the crew of 1,400 aboard *Hood* survived. Every Royal Navy unit available was then given the task of destroying the *Bismarck*.

Force H set sail from Gibraltar to intercept the Bismarck with the aircraft carrier *Ark Royal*, battlecruiser *Renown* and light cruiser *Sheffield*. Despite the loss of *Hood*, *Bismarck* did not come out of the Denmark Strait engagement completely unscathed. A shell from *Prince of Wales* had ruptured the ship's fuel tanks, causing her to lose oil. The commerce raiding cruise was thus cut short, and the ship headed for the French port of Brest. *Bismarck* was temporarily lost to the Royal Navy after she evaded the radar of the shadowing cruisers *Suffolk* and *Norfolk*. She was found again, but the only way of stopping her was if something slowed the ship down. To try and do this, *Ark Royal* launched a strike with her Fairey Swordfish torpedo bombers. However, the aircrews were wrongly informed of the location of *Sheffield* and attacked her instead, thinking her to be *Bismarck*. The torpedoes that the Swordfish had dropped carried a new type of magnetic detonator which proved too unreliable. A second strike was flown carrying the older, and totally reliable, contact detonator. *Bismarck* was found and a torpedo wrecked her steering gear. Unable to evade the British ships closing in, the German battleship was destroyed by a force including *King George V* and *Rodney*.

Britain at rock bottom

The end of 1941 saw the nadir of British naval fortunes in the Mediterranean. The Mediterranean Fleet lost its aircraft carrier to bomb damage, had one battleship sunk off Crete and its two remaining battleships put out of action by Italian human torpedoes. Force H in its turn suffered as well: *Ark Royal* was sunk by *U-81* in November 1941. It was only the lack of action by the Italians that prevented a complete disaster for British fortunes.

1942 opened on a low note. The most urgent task during the first part of the year was supplying Malta. The island had been under heavy attack for many months, and supply convoys had to be very heavily escorted to stand any chance of getting through. Enough succeeded that Malta was kept from starving, but it was very close. The most heavily escorted convoy in the whole of the Second World War was the key to this. In August, Operation Pedestal was mounted which lead to enough supplies being sent to the island to keep it going.

Amphibious assaults and the end of Force H

Force H was not actually extant for a portion of 1942. It was stripped bare in May to provide ships for the assault on Vichy French forces at Diego Suarez in Madagascar during Operation Ironclad. This operation succeeded, but many argue that it was a waste of British naval resources at a critical time in the war.

November saw the turning point of the conflict. Operation Torch saw British and American forces landed in Morocco and Algeria under the British First Army. Force H was reinforced to cover these landings. The two main threats were the Italian fleet and French forces. In the end, only French forces fought, and the most significant battles took place at Casablanca where only American naval units were supporting operations.

The end of the campaign in North Africa saw an interdiction effort on a vast scale. The aim was to cut Tunisia completely off from Axis support. It succeeded and 250,000 men surrendered to 18th Army Group; an equal number to those who surrendered at Stalingrad. Force H again provided heavy cover for this operation.

Two further sets of landings were covered by Force H against interference from the Italian fleet. Operation Husky in July 1943 saw the invasion and conquest of Sicily, and Operation Avalanche saw an attack on the Italian mainland at Salerno.

Following the Allied landings on Italy itself, the Italian government surrendered. The Italian fleet mostly escaped German capture and much of it formed the Italian Co-Belligerent Navy. However, two German Fritz X radio-controlled missiles did hit and sink the battleship *Roma*, killing the Commander-in-Chief of the Italian Royal Navy (*Regia Marina*), Admiral Carlo Bergamini.

Force H met the Italian fleet near Sardinia and escorted it to Malta. Admiral Cunningham sent a very traditional signal to the Admiralty in London:
"Be pleased to inform their Lordships that the Italian fleet lies under the guns of the fortress at Malta."
With the surrender of the Italian fleet, the need for heavy units in the Mediterranean disappeared. The battleships and aircraft carriers of Force H dispersed to the Home Fleet and Eastern Fleet and the command was disbanded. Naval operations in the Mediterranean from now on would be conducted by lighter units.

Modern Force H

Today the only Royal Navy ships attached to Gibraltar and the Western Mediterranean is the Gibraltar Squadron.

Battles and Operations of Force H

- Action at Oran (Operation 'Catapult') - 3 July 1940
- Battle of Calabria - 9 July 1940
- Attack on Taranto (Operation 'Judgement') - 11/12 November 1940
- Battle of Cape Spartivento - 27 November 1940
- Malta Convoy (Operation 'Collar') - November 1940
- Malta Convoy (Operation 'Excess') - January 1941
- Naval bombardment of Genoa (Operation 'Grog') - 9 February 1941
- Malta Convoy (Operation 'Substance') - July 1941
- Malta Convoy (Operation 'Halberd') - September 1941
- Malta Convoy (Operation 'Harpoon') - June 1942
- Malta Convoy (Operation 'Pedestal') - August 1942
- Invasion of Sicily (Operation 'Husky') - July 1943
- Invasion of Italy (Operation 'Avalanche') - September 1943

List of capital ships in Force H

- *Ark Royal*, aircraft carrier
- *Eagle*, aircraft carrier
- *Illustrious*, aircraft carrier
- *Hood*, battlecruiser (June-August 1940)
- *Resolution*, battleship (June-August 1940)
- *Valiant*, battleship (June 1940-December 1941, June-October 1943)
- *Renown*, battlecruiser (August 1940-August 1941, October 1941-February 1943)
- *Nelson*, battleship (June-September 1941, August 1942-November 1943)
- *Rodney*, battleship (May 1942-October 1943)
- *King George V*, battleship (May 1943-February 1944)
- *Enterprise*, cruiser (June-December 1940)
- *Arethusa*, cruiser (June 1940-December 1941)
- *Sheffield*, cruiser (August 1940-October 1941)
- *Coventry*, cruiser (August 1940-September 1942)
- *Calcutta*, cruiser (August 1940-June 1941)
- *Berwick*, cruiser (November 1940)
- *Fiji*, cruiser (April-May 1941)
- *Hermione*, cruiser (June 1941-March 1942)
- *Cairo*, cruiser (January-August 1942)
- *Charybdis*, cruiser (April-November 1942)
- *Argonaut*, cruiser (October-December 1942)

Source (edited): "http://en.wikipedia.org/wiki/Force_H"

Force K

Force K was a British Royal Navy task force of the Second World War. Initially, it was based in Freetown, Sierra Leone, and hunted German commerce raiders in the South Atlantic. It consisted of the battlecruiser *Renown*, the aircraft carrier *Ark Royal*, which were escorted by the destroyers, *Hardy*, *Hostile*, *Hereward*, and *Hasty*. After the Battle of the River Plate in December 1939, it was sent to Montevideo, Uruguay, to reinforce the ships blockading the damaged German pocket battleship *Admiral Graf Spee*.

It operated out of Malta and was responsible for intercepting convoys carrying supplies to the Italian and German forces in North Africa, including Erwin Rommel's *Afrika Korps*.

Force K was created on 21 October 1941 following Operation Sunflower, the German invasion of North Africa in the Spring of 1941. Allied submarines and aircraft could not inflict significant damage to Axis convoys supplying their forces in Africa, so Winston Churchill established Force K. At its inception, the Force consisted of the cruisers *Aurora* and *Penelope* and the L-class destroyers *Lance* and *Lively*.

In November 1941, Force K successfully destroyed an entire Axis convoy, forcing the Italians to consider Tripoli "practically blockaded". Soon after, Force K was reinforced by the arrival in Malta of Force B with two light cruisers—*Ajax* and *Neptune*—and two K-class destroyers. These were so effective that during November 1941 the Axis supply line suffered 60% losses. However on 19 December 1941 ships from both Forces ran into a minefield while pursuing an Italian convoy. Mines sank *Neptune* and damaged *Aurora*. The destroyer *Kandahar* was also mined while attempting to assist the stricken *Neptune*. The damaged *Kandahar* was scuttled the next day by the destroyer *Jaguar*.

Following this, and with a resurgence of the aerial bombardment of Malta, surface ships were withdrawn from there. Only *Penelope* remained, as she was too damaged to leave. Frequent air attacks while she remained in harbour earned her the nickname "HMS Pepperpot". She was eventually withdrawn, ending Force K's deployment, for the time being.

In November 1942, after the effective resupply convoys of Operations *Pedestal* and *Stoneage*, Force K was reinstated. Cruisers *Dido* and *Euryalus* and the 14th Destroyer Flotilla were detached from the *Stoneage* convoy and based at Malta.

Source (edited): "http://en.wikipedia.org/wiki/Force_K"

Force Z

Force Z was an Allied naval detachment consisting of the battleship HMS *Prince of Wales*, the battlecruiser HMS *Repulse*, and four destroyers, HMS *Electra*, *Express*, *Encounter*, and HMS *Jupiter*. Initially an aircraft carrier HMS Indomitable was included, but she ran aground in the Caribbean, and was not replaced by HMS Hermes which was regarded as too slow.

A renamed Force G, Force Z arrived at Singapore on 2 December 1941. It was sent to intercept Japanese landings in Malaya. *Prince of Wales* and *Repulse* were sunk by Japanese air attack on 10 December 1941.

After the attack on Pearl Harbor, Japanese forces mobilized everywhere with the task of eliminating opposition to the empire. Force Z happened to be caught with-in Japanese territory at the time. This lead the fleet to be a prime target for Japanese military forces in the Pacific. Without air cover and reinforcements, Force Z had little to defend itself with against the air assault by Japanese forces.

Source (edited): "http://en.wikipedia.org/wiki/Force_Z"

Home Fleet

The **Home Fleet** was a fleet of the Royal Navy which operated in the United Kingdom's territorial waters from 1902 with intervals until 1967.

Pre–World War I

On 1 October 1902, the Admiral Superintendent Naval Reserves, then Vice-Admiral Gerard Noel, was given the additional appointment of Commander-in-Chief, Home Fleet, and allotted a Rear Admiral to serve under him as commander of the Home Squadron. '...the nucleus of the Home Fleet would consist of the four Port Guard ships, which would be withdrawn from their various scattered dockyards and turned into a unified and permanent sea-going command – the Home Squadron – based on Portland. Also under the direction of the commander-in-chief of the Home Fleet would be the Coast Guard ships, which would continue to be berthed for the most part in their respective district harbours in order to carry out their local duties, but would join the Home Squadron for sea work at least three times per year, at which point the assembled force – the Home Squadron and the Coast Guard vessels – would be known collectively as the Home Fleet.' HMS *Empress of India* became flagship for Rear Admiral George Atkinson-Willes, commanding the Home Squadron.

On 14 December 1904 the Channel Fleet was re-styled the Atlantic Fleet and the Home Fleet became the Channel Fleet. In 1909 the Home Fleet was re-formed with Admiral Sir William May in command. He was succeeded in 1911 by Admiral Sir George Callaghan. On 4 August 1914, as the First World War was breaking out, John Jellicoe was ordered to take command of the Fleet, which by his appointment order was renamed the Grand Fleet.

The name "Home Fleet" was resurrected in March 1932, as the new name for the Atlantic Fleet, following the Invergordon Mutiny. The Commander-in-Chief, Home Fleet in 1933 was Admiral Sir John Kelly, GCVO, KCB. The Home Fleet comprised the flagship HMS *Nelson* leading a force which included the 2nd Battle Squadron (United Kingdom) (five more battleships), the Battlecruiser Squadron (HMS Hood and HMS Renown), the Second Cruiser Squadron (three), three destroyer flotillas (27), a submarine flotilla (six), two aircraft carriers and associated vessels.

Commanders in-Chief During the Inter War Period were:
- Admiral Sir John Kelly (1932–1933)
- Admiral Sir William Boyle (1933–1935)
- Admiral Sir Roger Backhouse (1935–1938)

Second World War

The Home Fleet was the Royal Navy's main battle force in European waters during the Second World War. On 3 September 1939, under Admiral Forbes flying his flag in HMS *Nelson* at Scapa Flow, it consisted of the 2nd Battle Squadron, the Battle Cruiser Squadron, 18th Cruiser Squadron, Rear-Admiral, Destroyers, Rear-Admiral, Submarines (2nd Submarine Flotilla, Dundee, 6th

Submarine Flotilla, Blyth, Northumberland), Vice-Admiral, Aircraft Carriers (Vice Admiral L.V. Wells, with HMS *Ark Royal*, HMS *Furious*, and HMS *Pegasus*), and the Orkney and Shetlands force. Its chief responsibility was to keep the German Navy from breaking out of the North Sea. For this purpose the First World War base at Scapa Flow was reactivated as it was well-placed for interceptions of ships trying to run the blockade.

The two most surprising losses of the Home Fleet during the early part of the war were the sinking of the old battleship HMS *Royal Oak* by the German submarine *U-47* while supposedly safe in Scapa Flow and the loss of the pride of the Navy, the battlecruiser HMS *Hood*, to the German battleship *Bismarck*.

The operational areas of the Home Fleet were not circumscribed, and units were detached to other zones quite freely. However the southern parts of the North Sea and the English Channel were made separate commands for light forces, and the growing intensity of the Battle of the Atlantic led to the creation of Western Approaches Command. Only with the final destruction of the *Tirpitz* in 1944 did the Home Fleet assume a lower priority, and most of its heavy units were withdrawn to be sent to the Far East.

Commanders-in-Chief during the Second World War were:
- Admiral Sir Charles Forbes (1939–1940),
- Admiral Sir John Tovey (1940–1942),
- Admiral Sir Bruce Fraser (1942–1944)
- Admiral Sir Henry Moore (14 June 1944–24 November 1945)

Post-Second World War

After the Second World War, the Home Fleet took back all of its peacetime responsibilities for the Royal Navy forces in home waters and also in the North and South Atlantic. With the Cold War, greater emphasis was placed on protecting the North Atlantic from the Soviet Union in concert with other countries as part of NATO.

Admiral Sir Rhoderick McGrigor took command of the Fleet in 1948 from Admiral Edward Syfret and in June–July 1949 supervised combined Western Union exercises involving ships from the British, French, and Netherlands Navies. Admiral McGrigor flew his flag from the aircraft carrier HMS *Implacable*. Also taking part in the exercises was HMS *Victorious* and HMS *Anson* along with cruisers and destroyers. During the exercise the combined force paid a visit to Mount's Bay in Cornwall from 30 June to 4 July 1949. Admiral Sir Philip Vian was Commander-in-Chief from 1950 to 1952, flying his flag in HMS *Vanguard*.

The Commander-in-Chief, Home Fleet, gained an additional NATO responsibility as Commander-in-Chief, Eastern Atlantic, as part of SACLANT, when the NATO military command structure was established in 1953 at the Northwood Headquarters in northwest London. The Commander-in-Chief Home Fleet still flew his flag however in HMS Tyne at Portsmouth. During Exercise Mainbrace in 1952, NATO naval forces came together for the first time to practice the defence of northern Europe; Denmark and Norway. The resulting McMahon Act difficulties caused by potential British control of the United States Navy's attack carriers armed with nuclear weapons led to the creation of a separate Striking Fleet Atlantic, directly responsible to the commander of the U.S. Navy's Atlantic Fleet, in his NATO position as SACLANT, by the end of 1952. In early January 1954 Admiral Sir Michael Denny took over as Commander-in-Chief, Home Fleet from Admiral Sir George Creasy.

In 1960 C-in-C Home Fleet moved to Northwood and in 1966 the NATO Channel Command (a post also held by C-in-C Home Fleet) moved to Northwood from Portsmouth. In 1963 Admiral Sir Charles Madden took command. In April 1963 the naval unit at the Northwood Headquarters was commissioned as HMS Warrior under the command of the then Captain of the Fleet. The Home Fleet was amalgamated with the Mediterranean Fleet in 1967. With its area of responsibility greatly increased and no longer being just responsible for the defence of home waters of the UK, the name of the fleet was changed to the Western Fleet, consigning the famous, historic name of the Home Fleet to history. Admiral Sir John Frewen had taken command of the Fleet from Admiral Madden in 1965 and was the Fleet's last Commander-in-Chief.

Flag Officers in the Home Fleet in the 1950s and 1960s included:
- Flag Officer, Training Squadron (HMS *Victorious* 1948-1950, 1954 spring cruise included HMS Implacable and HMS Indefatigable)
- Flag Officer, Heavy Squadron (Rear-Admiral Caspar John 1951-52, Vice Admiral John Hughes-Hallett 1952-53) - included HMS Vanguard?
- Flag Officer Flotillas, Home Fleet - flew flag in HMS Tyne, July 1960-March 1961

Commanders-in-Chief after the Second World War were:
- Admiral Sir Edward Syfret (1945–1948)
- Admiral Sir Rhoderick McGrigor (1948–1950)
- Admiral Sir Philip Vian (1950–1952)
- Admiral Sir George Creasy (1952–1954)
- Admiral Sir Michael Denny (1954–1955)
- Admiral Sir John Eccles (1955–1958)
- Admiral Sir William Davis (1958–1960)
- Admiral Sir Wilfrid Woods (1960–1963)
- Admiral Sir Charles Madden (1963–1965)
- Admiral Sir John Frewen (1965–1967)

Source (edited): "http://en.wikipedia.org/wiki/Home_Fleet"

List of Eastern Fleet ships

The Eastern Fleet was a World War II formation of the British Royal Navy. It was formed from the ships and installations of the East Indies Station and the China Station (which are included in this list), with headquarters at Singapore, moving between Trincomalee and Kilindini after the Japanese advances in south east Asia made Singapore untenable as a naval base. See main article for details.

The following lists the warships and support ships of the Fleet, with dates served, fate and nationality.
Source (edited): "http://en.wikipedia.org/wiki/List_of_Eastern_Fleet_ships"

Mediterranean Fleet

The British **Mediterranean Fleet** was part of the Royal Navy. The Fleet was one of the most prestigious commands in the navy for the majority of its history, defending the vital sea link between the United Kingdom and the majority of the British Empire in the Eastern Hemisphere. The first Commander-in-Chief, Mediterranean, may have been named as early as 1665, and the Fleet was in existence until 1967.

Pre-Second World War

In the last decade of the nineteenth century, the Mediterranean Fleet was the largest single squadron of the Royal Navy, with ten first-class battleships - double the number in the Channel Fleet - and a large number of smaller vessels. In 1893, Vice-Admiral Sir George Tryon drowned when his flagship, HMS *Victoria*, collided with HMS *Camperdown*, and sank within fifteen minutes.

Of the three original *Invincible*-class battlecruiser which entered service in the first half of 1908, two (HMS *Inflexible* and *Indomitable*) joined the Mediterranean Fleet in 1914. They and HMS *Indefatigable* formed the nucleus of the fleet at the start of the First World War when British forces pursued the German ships *Goeben* and *Breslau*.

A recently-modernised HMS *Warspite* became the flagship of the Commander-in-Chief and Second-in-Command, Mediterranean Fleet in 1926.

The Mediterranean Fleet achieved an especially high degree of professional excellence under the leadership of Admiral Roger Keyes from 1926 to 1929. He had under his command such strong figures as Dudley Pound as Chief of Staff, *Ginger* Boyle, commanding a cruiser squadron and Augustus Agar, V. C. commanding a destroyer flotilla.

Second World War

Malta, as part of the British Empire from 1814, was a shipping station and was the headquarters for the Mediterranean Fleet until the mid-1930s. Due to the perceived threat of air-attack from the Italian mainland, the fleet was moved to Alexandria, Egypt shortly before the outbreak of the Second World War. This decision contributed to the continuing ability of the Fleet to sustainably fight against the Axis forces.

Sir Andrew Cunningham took command of the fleet from HMS *Warspite* on 3 September 1939, and under him the major formations of the Fleet were the 1st Battle Squadron, 1st Cruiser Squadron, 3rd Cruiser Squadron, Destroyers, and the aircraft carrier HMS *Glorious*.

In 1940, the Mediterranean Fleet successfully attacked the Italian Fleet at Taranto by air. Other major actions included the Battle of Cape Matapan, and the Battle of Crete. The Fleet had to block Italian and later German reinforcements and supplies for the North African Campaign.

Post war

In October 1946, HMS *Saumarez* hit a mine in the Corfu Channel, starting a series of events known as the Corfu Channel Incident. The channel was cleared in 'Operation Recoil' the next month, involving 11 minesweepers under the guidance of HMS *Ocean*, two cruisers, three destroyers, and three frigates.

In May 1948, Sir Arthur Power took over as Commander-in-Chief Mediterranean, and in his first act arranged a show of force to discourage the crossing of Jewish refugees into Palestine. When later that year Britain pulled out of the British Mandate of Palestine, HMS *Ocean*, four destroyers, and two frigates escorted the departing High Commissioner, aboard the cruiser HMS *Euryalus*. The force stayed to cover the evacuation of British troops into the Haifa enclave and south via Gaza. In July 1947, after the main force, headed by two carriers, *Ocean* and *Triumph*, had visited Istanbul, HM Ships *Liverpool*, HMS *Chequers*, and *Chaplet* visited Sevastopol.

The battleship *Vanguard* briefly served with the Fleet in 1949 for six months. *Vanguard* was back in the Mediterranean briefly in 1954 during combined exercises with the Home Fleet.

From 1952 until 1967, the post of Commander in Chief Mediterranean Fleet was given a dual-hatted role as NATO Commander in Chief of Allied Forces Mediterranean in charge of all forces assigned to NATO in the Mediterranean Area. The British made strong representations within NATO in discussions regarding the development of the Mediterranean NATO command structure, wishing to retain their direction of NATO naval command in the Mediterranean to protect their sea lines of communication running through the Mediterranean to the Middle East and Far East. When a NATO naval commander, Admiral Robert B. Carney, C-in-C Allied Forces Southern Europe, was appointed, relations with the incumbent British C-in-C, Admiral Sir John Edelsten, were frosty. Edlesten, on making an apparently friendly offer of the use of communications facilities to Carney, who initially lacked secure communications facilities, was met with 'I'm not about to play Faust to your Mephistopheles through the medium of communications!'

In 1956, ships of the Fleet took part in the Suez War against Egypt.

From 1957 to 1959, Rear Admiral Charles Madden held the post of Flag Officer Malta, with responsibilities for three squadrons of minesweepers, an amphibious warfare squadron, and a flotilla of submarines stationed at the bases around Valletta Harbour. In this capacity, he had to employ considerable diplomatic skill to maintain good relations with Dom Mintoff, the nationalistic prime minister of Malta.

In the 1960s, as the importance of maintaining the link between the United Kingdom and British territories and commitments East of Suez decreased as the Empire dismantled, and the focus of Cold War naval responsibilities moved to the North Atlantic, the Mediterranean Fleet was gradually drawn down, finally disbanding in June 1967. Eric Groves, in *Vanguard to Trident*, details how by the mid-1960s the permanent strength of the Fleet was 'reduced to a single small escort squadron [appears to have been 30th Escort Squadron with HMS *Brighton*, HMS *Cassandra*, HMS *Aisne* plus another ship] and a coastal minesweeper squadron.' Deployments to the Beira Patrol and elsewhere reduced the escort total in 1966 from four to two ships, and then to no frigates at all. The Fleet's assets and area of responsibility were given to the new Western Fleet. As a result of this change, the UK relinquished the NATO post of Commander in Chief Mediterranean, which was disbanded.

The Royal Navy often deploys a warship to the NATO multi-national squadron Standing NATO Maritime Group 2, the NATO successor to Standing Naval Force Mediterranean.

Commanders in Chief of the Mediterranean Fleet

Commanders-in-Chief have included: Source (edited): "http://en.wikipedia.org/wiki/Mediterranean_Fleet"